I0103209

EVERYONE WINS!

EVERYONE WINS!

PLAYING THE GAME
OF
CONFLICT RESOLUTION
IN
ALL YOUR RELATIONSHIPS

Lawrence Barkan

Everyone Wins

©2006, Lawrence Barkan. All rights reserved.

No part of this book, either in part or in whole, may be reproduced, transmitted or utilized in any form or by any electronic, photographic or mechanical means, including photocopying, recording, or entry into any information storage and retrieval system without permission in writing from the copyright owner, by way of the publisher, except for brief quotations embodied in literary articles and reviews.

ISBN 13: 978-0-911041-69-9
ISBN 10: 0-911041-69-9

Book design: Optimum Performance Associates
Published by OPA Publishing, Chandler, Arizona

For permissions, serialization, condensations or adaptations, write to the publisher's address, below:

OPA Publishing, Box 1764, Chandler, Arizona 85244-1764

Printed in the United States of America

Table of Contents

Acknowledgments: With Gratitude i

Introduction: Some Thoughts About the Game iii

Chapter 1: The Rules of the Game 1

Chapter 2: Give Up Your Need To Be Right, Not Your Needs 11

Chapter 3: Take It Or Leave It Is Not Conflict,
  It's An Ultimatum 21

Chapter 4: You Can't Always Get What You Want,
  But You Can Always Get What You Need 31

Chapter 5: To Play Or To Pass: That is the Question 41

Chapter 6: With Whom Should I Play The Game? 49

Chapter 7: Time Out: Plan to Celebrate
  Everyone Winning the Game 55

Chapter 8: Step 1: The Opening Moves 63

Chapter 9: Time Out: Express Appreciation 75

Chapter 10: Step 2: Listening: The "Judo"
  of the Conflict Game 81

Chapter 11: Time Out: Have You Been Fully Understood? 101

Chapter 12: Step 3: Bridging: Playing To Collaborate
  Rather Than To Compete 107

Chapter 13: Step 4: Brainstorming: There Are Many Ways
  For Everyone To Win the Game 121

Chapter 14: Step 5: Choose "Everyone Wins" Solution(s) 131

Chapter 15: Celebrate the Victory 139

Chapter 16: You Must Keep Practicing
  For Everyone to Keep Winning 145

About the Author

Acknowledgments

With Gratitude

"No man is an island entire of itself . . . Therefore,
never send to know for whom the bell tolls,
it tolls for thee."

Meditation XVII
John Donne, English poet and clergyman - 1572-1631

After I completed the manuscript for this book, I sent it to friends and colleagues and asked for their critiques. Secretly, I hoped they would tell me that they were recommending the book for the next Pulitzer. Thankfully, they loved me enough to tell me I wasn't quite ready for that award. Their feedback has been invaluable, and I've incorporated much of it into this book. Some feedback I didn't use—and I hope they'll continue to love me anyway.

So here's some tolling of the bells for those who have been so generous to me:

To Michael Nees, business colleague and friend: Many of the concepts in this book were developed with Michael and I'm in indebted to him for his unselfish contributions including the diagram of the "Everyone Wins" process that appears on page 42. Without prompting, Michael would contact me with new ideas for improving the book. You are a generous spirit who has contributed immeasurably to my development.

i

To Kathy Carroll, Michael's wife: Their critiques arrived together in a single document. It was delightful to read Michael's comments, followed by Kathy's comments followed by Michael's comments, followed by Kathy's comments, and so on. The two of you deserve each other, and I mean that in the sense of the great gift you are for each other. I hope you think I deserve you.

To Robin Johnstone, my dear friend and mentor: Whenever my emotions got the best of me and I was absolutely convinced that I was right and everyone else was wrong, Robin would listen and help me sort through the rubbish of my thinking. I'd end up laughing at myself, which is the best tonic for getting back to work with a clear mind. I love you.

To Dan Springer: I first met Dan in a seminar Michael and I taught seven years ago. Dan read the manuscript and spent over six hours with me going through his feedback point by point. And all this as he was about to take on the presidency of a company! I'm in your debt.

To Carolyn and Cliff Wilkerson: You are an inspiration to me. I hope, one day, to grow up to be just like you. Thanks for the feedback, thanks for the love, and thanks for having an open door policy when Carol and I are in Chicago.

Finally, to Carol Barkan: What can I say, my darling? You gave me honest feedback even when I'd rather not have heard it; encouragement when all I wanted to do was give up; and unconditional love even when I didn't deserve it. I love you. Why you love me will always remain one of the mysteries of my life.

Some Thoughts About the Game

Welcome to the game of conflict and conflict resolution. It's a game process I've been teaching people to play for almost 20 years and I'm looking forward to sharing my excitement with you.

I teach techniques for conflict resolution to groups of (usually) about 20 people at a time. Typically, they are seated around tables that are arranged in a U-shape. This time, however, instead of being one of 20 people, you are in a class by yourself— and I am your personal instructor.

I promise that after reading this book you will be able to resolve your conflicts. If not, please contact me and I will give you your money back. Honest. Just send me an e-mail outlining what didn't work (and why, if you can figure that out). My online address is: ljbarkan@thepivotalfactor.com

I can make that promise because I know that resolving your conflicts is completely within your control. Does that surprise you? You've probably been thinking that some conflicts are impossible to resolve because the people with whom you're in conflict are being "impossible".

But there's something common to every conflict in which you're involved, and becoming aware of this commonality will make all the difference. In Chapter 1, I'll tell you what that is.

As you get ready to play this game, it's important for you to consider what **must** happen for you to be **delighted** by your decision to invest your money and time in this book. After all, if you commit to playing the game of conflict, you're spending dollars and hours that could be allocated to doing other things. You should expect to be delighted in return for your investment. But of course you need to give some thought to the reasons you picked up this book in the first place, because the clearer you can be as to what you want, the more likely it is that you will get it.

You may be reading because you're thinking of a specific situation that has been troubling you for some time. Or perhaps you want to find a way to handle a person who has been difficult to get along with. Perhaps conflict is simply a topic you want to learn more about. Pause for a moment and consider the best possible outcome that could occur as a result of your playing the game of conflict.

It may surprise you to think of conflict as a game. Such serious issues in your life may seem like anything but a game. Your particular conflicts may seem too stressful, too exhausting and too discouraging to be thought of as frameworks for a game. But hear me out.

In a conflict, as in a game, there is a strategy, there are moves and countermoves, and there is something at stake (getting your needs met and strengthening the relationships with the people with whom you're at odds). I will address all of these aspects as we go along.

In fact, in the game that I'm asking you to play, "winning" means three things:

- that you get your needs met;
- that the people with whom you're in conflict get their needs met, as well; and

- that, because of these positive personal outcomes, the level of trust between you increases and relationships are strengthened.

You may be thinking that games are only fun when there are winners and losers. In fact, you may think that what makes a game exciting is the possibility that you will win (or lose) and the other people playing the game will lose (or win).

However, unlike a competitive game, in which there is a winner and a loser, *everyone* will win the game of conflict if you play it as I will encourage you to do.

Imagine what your life might be like, for example, if you lived a life of collaboration rather than one of conflict—a life in which there are only winners and you don't have to continually look over your shoulder, fearing that even though you may have won this time you could lose the next time. Even more to the point, imagine a life in which conflicts can be a source of creativity rather than a guarantee of stress. Might that be a game worth playing?

If you have come to this book thinking that you must defeat someone else and be declared the "winner" of the conflict, then I suggest you look elsewhere. There are hundreds of books designed to teach you how to beat others at whatever game you want to play. Besides, "winning" at that game requires constant vigilance lest your opponent find a way to beat you the next time. Trust actually decreases and relationships are harmed when that becomes the conflict game.

Like every game, resolving conflicts can be fun (yes, fun) if you take it very seriously by giving your whole self to the game. Do you remember playing good guys and bad guys (or with dolls and doll houses) as a child and pretending, with your whole being, that the game was real? A game is most fun when you forget it's a game and give your whole self to it. Therefore, I encourage you to approach this book with all the energy, passion and commitment that you might approach playing any game.

In order to fulfill on my promise that you will be able to resolve *any* conflict, you must make two agreements with me and you must maintain these agreements at least for the remainder of this book.

The first agreement I'm requesting from you is that you allow me to be your coach. For me, coaching means "interrupting". If I'm a successful coach, I'll interrupt your usual way of thinking and behaving. In fact, in my opinion, the only possible reason for you to read further is if you'll allow me to do so. After all, as I was told long ago, "If you always do what you've always done, you'll always get what you've always got." Or, to state it in the most obvious way possible, "Nothing changes until something changes."

You don't have to agree with my coaching. I am asking, however, that you accept it. "Acceptance" means that, for the remainder of this book, you will put aside your judgments and maintain an open mind.

Putting aside judgments and creating an open mind are the prerequisites to learning anything new—and they're the two most difficult things to actually accomplish. Be forewarned! As you progress through the book, you will almost instinctively want to filter what you're reading through the prism of what you already know and believe.

I'm not asking you to forget all that prior knowledge and experience. That would be impossible. I am, however, asking that you temporarily suspend what you know and believe and allow me to suggest possible new beliefs and present alternative ways of behaving.

The second agreement I want you to make with me is that you will do the assignments at the end of each chapter. These assignments are designed to help you look at the conflicts in your life and to alter both the way in which you see them and the way you generally behave as a result of this perception.

If you will accept these agreements, then the promise of this book will be fulfilled for you; you will resolve your conflicts, and you will strengthen your relationships.

On the other hand, if you cannot accept these agreements, then I suggest you read no further. You will not—cannot—realize the value from this book that I am committed you receive.

In Chapters 1 through 7, I'll guide you through a time of "Warming Up" to get you ready for the game. The information in these chapters consists of what you need to know to be successful when playing the game of conflict.

Chapters 8 through 14 ("Let the Games Begin") outlines, describes and exemplifies the steps involved in playing the game in such a way as to bring every conflict to a satisfactory conclusion.

Chapters 15 and 16 are, in effect, the "Post Game Wrap-Up." Chapter 15 encourages you to celebrate your "victories." Chapter 16 shows you how to ensure that what you learn and practice in this book will remain in your life-tools kit for the rest of your life.

The chart on page 42 displays the process steps that are covered in Chapters 5 through 15.

Every game has rest periods, so there are even some "time outs" in this game of conflict (Chapters 7, 9 and 11).

Before proceeding further, I want to make a few general recommendations that will increase your enjoyment of the game.

You may become so excited during "Warming Up" (Chapters 1 through 7) that you think you're ready to go out and play the game with the people with whom you're actually in conflict. I encourage you not to do that until you have read the entire book and have done the assignments that are recommended at the end of each chapter. I know this is a lot to ask. In your own, inevitably human way, you probably want to jump right in and resolve the conflicts in your life NOW. However, each chapter builds on the preceding ones. As you read, you will gain insights that will change your approach to your conflicts. It's quite probable that what you thought about conflict in Chapter 1 will be completely altered by the time you complete Chapter 16.

Just as I will be your coach as you navigate through these pages, I encourage you to ask someone in your life to be your real-time "coach" as you read and do the assignments.

How does your real-time coach help you? Well, imagine that you've made a commitment to get up every morning at 5 a.m. and exercise. When the alarm goes off at that unreasonably early hour, it's easy to find reasons to hit the snooze button—unless you know someone is waiting to exercise with you: your real-life coach.

Your coach will help you to hold to your promise to keep reading and practicing when all you want to do is quit. And, by the way, at some point you *will* want to quit, especially if you really are doing the assignments. Why might you find yourself wanting to quit?

We all have a little voice in our heads (call it that 5 a.m. exercise voice) that tells us how comfortable it is to keep doing what we're doing (like stay in bed or avoiding a conflict rather than dealing with it). Your coach will remind you that in this situation your "inner voice" is not your friend. That voice wants to keep you stuck.

Additionally, your coach is someone with whom you can discuss and practice the chapter assignments. It's often helpful to test the validity of what you think and believe with someone you trust.

Like me, your coach should be someone who will "interrupt" you. Select someone who is *not* convinced that the people with whom you are in conflict are behaving like "jerks". Rather, select someone who will tell you when *you're* behaving like a "jerk".

The examples I use throughout the book focus on two-person conflicts. But what if you engaged in conflicts that involve multiple persons or even several groups of people? Be assured that the skills you will need to be successful are the same in all cases. However, it may take longer to apply workable solutions in multiple-person conflicts simply because more people are involved and each personal situation may be different, so you may have to break the larger issues down into smaller ones and deal with each as a separate part of the whole.

Finally, I want to be gender neutral, so I will sometimes use "he" and sometimes use "she."

COACHING TIPS FROM THE INTRODUCTION:

1. **Keep your agreements: Be coachable and do the assignments at the end of every chapter.**

2. **Treat conflict like a game: Bring all of your energy, passion and commitment to this game.**

3. **Resist engaging in actual conflict resolution until you've read through the entire book.**

4. **Get a "real-time" coach who will hold you to your commitments.**

Part I: Warming Up

Chapter 1

The Rules of the Game

Every game has rules and the game of conflict is no different. There are two rules that must be understood before you begin playing.

RULE 1: CONFLICT = DISAGREEMENT

Have you ever noticed that the way you see something becomes the way it is for you? Consider these examples:

- Is your boss unreasonable in her demands, or is she just interested in excellence?

- Are employees being greedy when they're negotiating compensation, or are they concerned about the welfare of their families?

- Do you avoid giving feedback because you don't care, or are you hesitant because you're concerned about hurting the other person's feelings?

- Did your spouse not pick up the dry cleaning because he is getting back at you for something, or did he simply, legitimately forget?

- Is the waitress giving you slow service because she's incompetent, or is she being careful to make sure there are no mistakes in ordering with the kitchen?

- Is your daughter not cleaning her room because she wants to cause trouble, or does she just like her room that way (even though you clearly don't!)?

The way in which you choose to view these situations will dictate how you will respond. Depending on your perspective, you may be argumentative and angry, or you may choose to be accepting and generous.

Similarly, the way you choose to view a conflict will dictate how you will respond. Therefore, as your coach, I suggest that you think of conflict as nothing more than a disagreement. If, instead, you view conflict as some sort of battle in which there is a winner and a loser, I wouldn't be surprised if you avoided conflict (who wants to be in a war?) or acted aggressively in every confrontational situation (after all, who wants to lose?).

If you view conflict as simply a disagreement, then you might see the issue as presenting an opportunity rather than a problem. You might even begin to look forward to some conflicts because you realize that disagreements are often the very foundation of creative solutions to your problems.

Consider this: when someone disagrees with us, we have the opportunity to examine our beliefs, attitudes and behaviors. When someone disagrees with us, we have the opportunity to learn a new way—and perhaps a more effective one—of believing and behaving. If everyone in our life was in complete agreement with us, our relationships might go very smoothly, but there would be little opportunity or incentive for growth and development within each relationship.

My wife and I have disagreements, my business partners and I have disagreements, and my friends and I have disagreements. Heck, I read the newspaper and disagree with people I've never even met! All of these disagreements are potential opportunities for me to learn new ways of being and behaving.

Some of you, I know, have come to this book because you'd like to be able to *avoid* these disagreements. You think that your life would be happier if you could do so.

Unfortunately, it's an illusion to believe that you can avoid disagreements. You cannot. You may assiduously avoid having a conversation with the person with whom you disagree, but as a result you will keep the disagreement present in your life, either thinking about it to yourself or talking to your friends about it. Consider that it actually takes more energy (and saps more energy) to talk **about** people than to talk **to** them.

RULE 2: UNRESOLVED CONFLICT = DISAGREEMENT + THE NEED TO BE RIGHT

Rule 1 suggests that conflict is a creative opportunity for growth and development. Adding "the need to be right" to the equation turns conflict from an opportunity into a problem. "The need to be right" is what makes conflict so difficult to resolve.

My colleague, Michael Nees, defines the need to be right as "the rigid belief that your perspective is 'right'—the 'truth'—and there is no need to listen to other perspectives and only a need to argue and defend the 'rightness' of your position."

Let me give you an autobiographical example of this.

For much of my life, if I was in a conflict, I not only disagreed, I needed to be right in my disagreement. And not only did I **need** to be right, I **had** to be right! I demanded to be right! If the people with whom I disagreed didn't see things my way and I couldn't convince them otherwise, I talked about them behind their backs and tried to convince those I was talking to how right I was. I was being both disagreeing and disagreeable.

And at times I went the other way. I sulked, pouted and tried to avoid dealing with the disagreement. Of course, I could never really avoid the issue, because my sulking and pouting didn't make the disagreement disappear. All I was doing was making myself more miserable.

Then I had an insight that transformed my life and my relationships. The insight began, as I had begun, with my mother. I had a "cordial" relationship with my mother. She lived in Chicago and I lived in Phoenix, and I was glad for the distance. We'd talk on the telephone. I'd ask how she was feeling and about the weather. She'd say that it was cold in Chicago but that she had read in the paper that it was cold in Phoenix, as well. I confirmed that the mornings were colder than usual, but it warmed up nicely during the day.

In other words, we were acquaintances who happened to be related.

My friends knew about my relationship with my mother, and they were empathetic. After all, I had convinced them that she was argumentative, demanding, and had to be right about everything (of course, you'll recognize that this is exactly how I was behaving, but I didn't yet have that awareness). All my friends agreed that it was better for me to keep a physical and psychological distance from my mother.

Then one day my wife—from whom I learn a great deal because we disagree a great deal—asked me a question that transformed my relationship with my mother as well as with many others.

"Larry," she began, "I was thinking about your relationship with your mother, and I was thinking about your issues with me, and I was thinking about your problems with the people you tell me about at work, and it occurred to me that there's something common to everyone of those conflicts."

Always keen for some fresh insight, I asked eagerly, "What?"

"You," she said, and then she turned and walked away with a smile on her face.

"What?" I asked. "What do you mean?"

But in that very moment I knew exactly what she meant!

I was the common denominator at every one of those conflicts. The **content** of the conflicts was always different, depending on whom I was disagreeing with. Of course, the people involved were often different, but *I* was the person common to every conflict.

This insight is why I know, as I wrote in the introduction, "resolving conflict is within your (and my) control." Every conflict is different, every person in those conflicts is different, but **you** are present in every single situation. There's only one person in any conflict who must alter his behavior in order to resolve the conflict, and that's the person whose eyes you open every morning.

After all those years, I realized, as my wife was walking away, that it was my need to be right that was preventing me from resolving the conflicts in my life.

I had always thought that if I gave up my need to be right, I would lose and the other person would win. Now I was beginning to see that it was my need to be right itself that was preventing me from ever winning. You'll recall that winning in the game of conflict means that everyone gets his needs met and that this satisfaction strengthens the relationship itself. It finally came to me that there was no way I could win as long as I was intent on making sure that the other person lost.

I am most emphatically not suggesting that you give up getting your needs met. I am, however, equally emphatically saying that, likewise, no resolution of conflict is possible without your willingness to give up your need to be right. Do so and you can resolve the conflict; fail to do so and the conflict may never be resolved.

When my wife made her observation, I didn't immediately jump in the air and holler "Eureka," delighted with her insight. In fact, I spent the next several weeks trying to convince my wife, my friends and anyone else I could that "Yes, I am present at every conflict, but that doesn't mean I am to blame for every conflict." Surely, I argued, my mother, my wife and my co-workers have to share at least some of the blame.

When I tried this argument out on my wife, she listened (with that serene smile on her face that can drive me crazy because it ushers in something that will cause me to have to consider giving up my need to be right), and then she said, "I'm not talking about blame. I'm talking about responsibility."

"And the difference is . . .?" I asked.

"The difference," she said "is that blame means you're wrong, while responsibility means you're free." And again she turned and walked away, leaving me to ponder this.

You may understand immediately what my wife meant. But it took me several weeks to "get it," to comprehend the power of what she said. Then I needed to spend several months of learning and practicing to eventually begin "living" it. This simple but profound change of attitude (and ultimately, belief) has made an enormous difference in my life. It forms the basis of the seminars I teach, the coaching I do, and the way I live my life. In fact, it's the reason this book exists.

What I came to realize was this: When we blame others for our problems, we become victims and other people become our masters; we are at their mercy. We must rely on them for resolution and, if they won't give us what we need, we grow resentful and make them wrong, and in the process we make ourselves wrong.

Conversely, when we take responsibility, we recognize that *we* are the source of the problems in our lives. But here's the good news: Even though we may have created our problems, we can fix them! We don't have to waste time blaming others and trying to convince everyone around us how "right" we are. We aren't stuck waiting for others to see that they are "wrong" and we are "right." Rather, we take action that allows for all of us to get our needs met. Giving up the need to be right is one of the most generous things you can do because it signals your willingness to see the legitimacy of all sides in a conflict.

This "aha" insight has given me the tremendous gift of a life in which conflict is a lot less stressful and is generally resolved fairly quickly. In fact, **the speed with which I resolve any conflict is directly proportional to how fast I am willing to give up my need to be right.**

For all of us to achieve this level of freedom, however, we have to utterly and completely give up our need to be right. I ask you to consider the possibility that it's not our mothers, friends, co-workers, bosses, wives, husbands, neighbors, etc. who are to blame for the conflicts in our lives. We are, at some level, responsible for those conflicts by our refusal to give up our need to be right. Shakespeare knew this hundreds of years ago when he wrote in *Julius Caesar,* "The fault, Dear Brutus, is not in our stars but in ourselves that we are underlings."

Failing to give up the need to be right is a virtual assurance that a conflict will be perpetuated. This will become much clearer to you in Chapter 10 when I discuss "Listening: The Judo of the Conflict Game."

One of the first actions I took after I really understood the power of this insight was to call my mother and apologize for the way I'd been with her my whole life.

"I'm the one who is argumentative, and I'm the one who has to be right all the time," I told her. "All these years I thought it was you, but it was me." For the first time in . . . maybe forever . . . my mother and I had a real conversation, and we established a real relationship. And just in time. My mother died two years later, by which time she knew how much I loved her and I knew how much she loved me.

In the next chapter, you'll see what it means to give up the need to be right, and Chapter 3 will address those times when it may not be appropriate to do so.

COACHING TIPS FROM CHAPTER 1:

1. *Conflict = Disagreement*, nothing more.

2. Conflict is a problem when we add "the need to be right" to the equation above.

3. Consider that the time it will take you to resolve any conflict is directly proportional to how fast you are willing to give up your need to be right.

CHAPTER 1 ASSIGNMENTS

Use the spaces below to do the following:

1. Write a list of the people with whom you have an unresolved conflict. Select people with whom the relationship is important. You're going to be working on these conflicts through the remainder of the book.

2. Beside each person, write words that describe your perception of him (or her). For example, you may think a person is "unreasonable" or "argumentative" or "difficult to get along with."

3. Consider that these ways of seeing people are examples of your need to be right about them and are what is keeping the conflict in place. Comment, if you wish, in the gray areas.

If you would rather not write in this book—either to keep it neat so you can hand it on to someone else who needs it or because you'd rather keep your thoughts and ideas private and confidential—you may copy the assignment pages for each chapter and/or do the optional assignments in a journal or on a note pad.

Person	Perception

Optional assignment: Write down your thoughts and feelings about your conflicts. You may choose to use the space below or to create a separate journal.

Remember: As your coach, I'm not asking you to agree with me. I am asking you to temporarily put aside your judgments and opinions and simply do the assignments.

TODAY'S DATE: _____

Thoughts and Feelings:

_____

_____

_____

_____

_____

_____

_____

_____

_____

_____

_____

_____

_____

_____

_____

_____

_____

_____

_____

_____

_____

Give Up Your Need
To Be Right,
Not Your Needs

The need to be right: "The rigid belief that your perspective is 'right'—the 'truth'—and there is no need to listen to other perspectives and only a need to argue and defend the 'rightness' of your position."

Michael Nees, Managing Partner,
The *Pivotal* Factor, LLC

Why is it so difficult to give up our need to be right? Each of us will have a different answer to that question. One answer that seems to apply to many of the people I've taught and coached is that they think that what they believe is not simply a point of view but is, in fact, "the truth". They refuse to give up their need to be right because they think they **are** right. Let me give you an example.

I was coaching a woman (let's call her Susan) who was encountering tremendous resistance to the change effort she was attempting to institute in her company. Susan was frustrated by the resistance and she asked me to help her understand why that was so and what to do about it.

The first few sessions I had with Susan were mostly spent with me listening to her complaints about the people who reported to her. I suggested that she allow me to contact these people so that I could learn more about why they were behaving in this way. She reluctantly agreed. She was convinced she knew the answer: the people who reported to her were to blame.

Using a survey that assured anonymity, I asked the people who reported to Susan why they were being resistant to her change initiative.

The answers that came back could all be grouped into several comments: "She's argumentative." "She doesn't listen." "She's hostile to our suggestions." The feedback was not a surprise to me. I had spent several hours with Susan, and this was my impression of her as well.

However, Susan was quite surprised by the feedback. After I had summarized what I learned, she said, "I don't see it," meaning that she didn't see herself in this way, to which I responded "Exactly. That's the problem. You don't see it."

I suggest that Susan's blind spot is one that many of us share. We don't see how our behavior is creating the very situation we say we want to solve. Susan believed it was the truth that the conflicts she was experiencing were the fault of the people who reported to her. She literally didn't see that this belief was the very thing keeping her from being successful.

After several coaching sessions, Susan became open to the possibility that her point of view about her employees was not the truth (that is, she gave up her need to be right). She started doing a lot more listening than demanding and, much to her surprise, the people who reported to her became far more co-operative. When she changed, they changed.

Susan's refusal to give up her need to be right created conflicts with her employees. Taken to an extreme, there are people who will literally kill others rather than give up the need to be right.

September 11th of 2001 is a terrifying reminder of that fact. While it's rare to find people who will kill us if we don't believe as they do (thank goodness), there are people who destroy relationships by their adamant and strident defense of their positions and their unwillingness to give up the need to be right. Are you one of them?

If you've believed something for a very long time ("my mother is . . ." "my boss is . . ." "my spouse is . . .") and you've been basing your behavior on that belief, it wouldn't be surprising for you to easily come to believe in the "rightness" of your belief and the "rightness" of your behavior. The surprise would be if you saw the world any differently.

Here's another example of a refusal to give up the need to be right.

I was coaching Jim, a manager who rarely gave positive feedback to the people who worked for him. As a result of my coaching, Jim started verbally praising employees who he had previously only criticized.

However, the employees, rather than thanking Jim for his new behavior, were extremely distrustful of the praise, and they often talked among themselves about how Jim would eventually, certainly, return to being critical. The employees had come to see this as "the truth" about Jim.

I'm not suggesting there weren't good reasons from the past for distrusting Jim's new behavior. After all, Jim had been critical for a long time before he changed.

I am suggesting, however, that unless those employees (and us when we find ourselves in similar situations) become willing to give up being right (from the past) and experiment with a new way of behaving (in the present), no resolution of conflict will be possible (in the future).

Giving up the need to be right requires that you:

1. **Listen: Be sure you *understand* <u>before</u> you give your opinion.**

I will have much more to say about listening in Chapter 10. "Listening for understanding" doesn't necessarily mean that you agree with the other person; it *does* mean that you are willing to really understand *why* the other person thinks and feels as she does. This was, basically, the coaching I gave to Susan.

2.   **Consider the possibility that many conflicts exist because of the judgments you have about people (and, of course, believing that your judgments are right).**

What might be possible if you approached your conflicts determined to understand why the person is behaving in a particular way before judging their behavior?

Recently, I was coaching Brenda, who had a brilliant engineer named Terry working for her. Many people relied on Terry for advice. However, people often avoided asking for his advice because he'd never give a direct answer. He would take so long to answer a question that people preferred not asking, even if it meant they might make a mistake.

When anyone attempted to give Terry this feedback, he'd get frustrated and even angry. More and more people were avoiding him. Brenda was upset with Terry and was even considering terminating him in spite of his technical expertise. Over a period of many weeks, she had conversations with Terry in which she told him he had to change "or else."

I gave Brenda some very simple coaching: I told her to ask Terry *"Why do you get so angry and frustrated?"* and then to *listen without judgment* to whatever he told her.

Brenda reported back to me that, once Terry realized she really wanted to understand and not to judge, he said that the reason he gave such long answers was because he was totally committed to giving away his knowledge. He really wanted to teach people so they could do things on their own, and he became angry and frustrated when they didn't seem to want to listen. In fact, at one time, he thought he might become a teacher because he so loved imparting his knowledge.

With this understanding, Brenda became much more compassionate towards Terry. She assured him that she understood and that she appreciated his desire to teach others. She coached Terry to control his anger and frustration and to learn to be more succinct in his answers. And Terry, who before had been resistant and even angry, accepted the coaching and changed his behavior. By being compassionate with Terry, Brenda was actually showing him how she wanted him to behave.

At last report, Terry was still teaching others, only now those others were grateful for the teaching.

3. Be open to the possibility that the other person is right.

It's important to remember that the other person is always right . . . *from his perspective.* If someone calls you a "jerk", you *are* a jerk . . . from his perspective. If someone says you're "difficult to get along with", you *are* difficult to get along with . . . from his perspective. Arguing with this perspective will only keep the conflict going.

I'm not suggesting that you agree with this person's assessment of you; rather, I am suggesting that you simply consider the possibility that—from his perspective—you're behaving in ways that cause him to think of you as a "jerk" and "difficult to get along with". All you need to do is "listen for understanding" to ensure that you know what you are doing that is causing the other person to see you in this way.

When you begin to accept the reality that the other person is always right (from his perspective), then you can quite easily give up getting into fruitless arguments about whose opinion is "more right" and start searching for creative ways to get everyone's needs met.

Here's an example of what I mean.

A few years ago, I was working with a team whose responsibility was to create and implement a web site for their company. The firm had been participating in Internet marketing in a small way but was about to take the plunge in a big and expensive way. As a result of this huge commitment, a lot was riding on the success of the team, and they were feeling the pressure. However, they were having difficulty moving the project forward because, when the team members gave each other feedback, the person receiving the feedback would become defensive. The team couldn't move forward because individual members were busy moving backwards, defending what they had just said. After some coaching, the team reduced the installation time for their company web site by six weeks.

And how were they able to create this breakthrough? Simple: I taught team members to accept the validity of the feedback they were receiving and to listen to understand the feedback without becoming defensive. Over time, all of the team's members learned and accepted that feedback (in both directions) was nothing more than information telling each other **exactly** what each person thought and believed, thus giving each other usable information upon which to make decisions about what needed to be done to make the entire team—and each of its members—most effective.

Before they worked with me, the members of the team would waste (not spend) great gobs of time defending their ideas and their behavior. After coaching, the members of the team would give each other feedback, asking "What do I need to do to change your perception?" If their suggestion was reasonable and appeared to be productive, they would . . . JUST DO IT! This simple change in behavior allowed the team to move forward more quickly than they ever thought possible.

I suggest to you that the people with whom you have unresolved conflicts are telling you **exactly** what you must do to be effective with them. However, you may not hear what they're saying because you're so busy defending yourself (that is, being right). **If this sounds too easy, you may be conditioned to believing that resolving conflict is hard. It isn't.** I've helped many teams and individuals do it and it's easy . . . once those teams and individuals accepted the reality that feedback is nothing more than information for them about the feedback giver and what they must do to be effective with that person. Instead of arguing about the truthfulness of someone's feedback to you, simply "listen to understand" the feedback. Your understanding of the feedback will give you access to your growth and development.

4. **Be open to the idea that there may be multiple ways to reach agreement and that your way may not be the only right way.**

There are always multiple ways for everyone to get their needs met, unless we decide that there aren't and demand that we be right. A simple way to determine if you are clinging to being right rather than open to multiple ways to reach agreement is to notice how many times you use the word "but" in a conversation. For example, you may find yourself saying to someone, "Automating many of our processes will save us money, but it will harm our reputation for customer service by taking away some of the human factor."

5. **Begin to replace the word "but" with the word "and."**

Michael Nees often says that "It's not a world of but . . . it's a world of and." I would amend that to say it's an "and, and, and, and world." For example, you might say, "Automating many of our processes will save us money **and** it will harm our reputation for customer service by taking away some of the human factor." When you use the word "but" you are, in effect, saying to the other person, "I'm going to prove to you why your idea is wrong." When you use the word "and," you are suggesting that the other person's ideas have merit **and** so do yours. Instead of arguing over who is "more right," the word "and" indicates that both of you are right and both sides must be considered when searching for creative solutions. "And" suggests it's not an unresolved conflict; it's simply a disagreement in search of various possible creative solutions.

COACHING TIPS FROM CHAPTER 2:

1. Your point of view is not the truth.

2. Giving up the need to be right means that you will:

    - *Listen to understand* before giving your opinion.

    - Be open to the possibility that the other person is right.

    - Be open to discovering multiple ways to reach agreement and not simply demanding that your way is the only "right way".

    - Notice yourself using the word "but," and replace it with the word "and".

CHAPTER 2 ASSIGNMENTS

Use the space below (or your private journal) to do the following:

1. Return to the assignment from Chapter 1 and review the names of the people with whom you are in an unresolved conflict.

2. Review the words you wrote to describe each person.

3. Use the space below to write down what might be possible if you gave up being right about each person.

For example, suppose you wrote "argumentative" next to a person's name. If you gave up seeing the person as being argumentative, you might be willing to consider why the person is being argumentative. You might begin to see that the person is being argumentative because you're being defensive. You might begin to see that if you gave up being defensive you might be able to have a meaningful conversation in which you really listened to the person. This listening might lead to a better relationship.

Name:	
What might change?	
Name:	
What might change?	
Name:	
What might change?	
Name:	
What might change?	
Name:	
What might change?	

Optional assignment: Write down your thoughts and feelings about your conflicts. You may choose to use the space below or to create a separate journal.

Remember: As your coach, I'm not asking you to agree with me. I am asking you to temporarily put aside your judgments and opinions and simply do the assignments.

TODAY'S DATE: _____

Thoughts and Feelings:

_____
_____
_____
_____
_____
_____
_____
_____
_____
_____
_____
_____
_____
_____
_____
_____
_____
_____
_____
_____
_____
_____
_____
_____

Chapter 3

Take It Or Leave It
Is Not Conflict,
It's An Ultimatum

After completing the assignments from Chapter 2, you may be thinking that there are some conflicts in which it's inappropriate to give up the need to be right because, in fact, you do need to be right.

For instance, you may have an employee who is consistently late, and tardiness is simply unacceptable. Or you may have a customer who demands delivery dates that are impossible to meet. Or you may have a boss who gives you assignments to complete at the last minute and there just isn't time to complete them by his deadline. Or you may have a co-worker who won't assist other team members and that behavior cannot be tolerated. Or you may have children who are continually threatening to quit school even though the law requires that they stay in school.

You may be feeling a lot of frustration about your specific situation. You probably think you've done everything but beg for the other person to change and nothing you've done has made any difference.

"Aren't there situations," you may ask, "where it's just inappropriate to give up the need to be right? Shouldn't I just tell people their behavior is unacceptable and demand that they change . . . or else? Aren't there situations where I just have to be right?"

My answer always is, "Yes, there are such situations. And what makes them difficult for you to deal with is that you treat these situations as though they were open to conflict resolution when, in fact, they are not. You keep seeking commitment when, in fact, all you really want is compliance. These situations are called *take it or leave it*. These are ultimatums and are not open to the "Everyone Wins" model. In these situations, not everyone will win because not everyone's needs will be met."

There are situations where it doesn't matter what the **other person's** needs are because no choice is possible. Either the other person complies with your request or suffers the consequences.

Likewise, there are situations where it doesn't matter what **your needs** are because no choice is possible. Either you comply with other's requests or *you* suffer the consequences. No conflict resolution is needed or called for. There is a rule or policy that must be adhered to, regardless of whether you like or agree with that rule or policy.

You must remember, however, that "being right" in these situations doesn't mean being righteous. "Being right" simply means that the decision is out of your hands and there's no point in talking further about it. You don't have to be angry, you don't have to be sarcastic, and you certainly don't have to be argumentative. All you have to do is present the ultimatum dispassionately.

As an example, let me tell you about Steve, a manufacturing superintendent.

At the time of the incident, the people who reported to Steve were new to him. At an introductory meeting, Steve requested that everyone comply with the company policy and wear a name badge to help Steve learn their names. The company actually required that everyone wear a badge, but only about 20% of the workforce was complying.

At 6:30 one morning, as Steve was getting coffee, an employee named Bill came up to Steve and, pointing to the badge on his (Bill's) chest, remarked sarcastically, "I want you to know I'm wearing the badge for you."

"For me?" Steve replied. "You don't have to wear that badge for me."

"I don't?" asked Bill, incredulously.

"No," Steve said. "You don't have to wear the badge at all. However, I'll miss you."

"Miss me?" asked Bill with surprise. "What do you mean?"

"Well," said Steve, "if you don't wear it, you can't work here. You're one of my very best people and I'll miss you." Steve made that statement without anger, sarcasm or argument.

After that, Bill wore the badge without complaint. He got the point. Do you?

In situations where the other person's commitment is desired, giving up the need to be right is appropriate and Chapters 8 to 14 will show you how to develop "Everyone Wins" solutions.

However, situations that require only compliance, such as the "Steve and Bill" situation related above, are *take it or leave it* ultimatums and don't really require much conversation at all.

For example, does your company have a policy that first shift workers must be ready to work by 8 AM? If you have an employee who is consistently late, that employee needs to be told that he can't work first shift anymore (or perhaps any shift, depending on the requirements of the other shifts).

Is your child old enough to quit school? If not, then she must be in school every day. It's the law. Why are you arguing with your child about going to school? You may want to talk about why she doesn't like school, but going to school doesn't require her commitment, only her compliance.

Is your "unreasonable" boss open to having a conversation about why you think he's unreasonable? If not, stop arguing with your boss. Your commitment isn't required, only your compliance. Either you will do what your boss demands or you may choose not to work there (*take it or leave it*). You might choose to go to Human Resources, or even your boss's boss, to get your needs met. However, stop expecting to get your needs met from your boss.

Does your spouse adamantly refuse to pick up her socks from the floor and put them in the clothes hamper? You have only one question to answer: Do you intend to stay married? If you do, stop expecting that she will pick up her socks. She won't. You must find another way to get your needs met (pick them up yourself, hire someone to do it, leave them there and refuse to wash them, etc.). Consider the possibility that if you continue to argue with your spouse about picking up her socks and you know she won't do it, then you must love arguing. Is it really worth it?

Does your co-worker refuse to assist you and others on the team? Give up expecting that he will, or go to your boss and ask her to take action with this person, but stop expecting to get co-operation from the offender himself. He is telling you by his behavior that he sees the issue as *take it or leave it*. You and the team will have to find other ways to get your needs met.

On one recent morning, when I was at a store getting some copying done and was standing at the counter waiting to pay, I overheard the conversation of the customer next to me.

The customer wanted the store employee to copy and bind a manual, and the employee was saying that he couldn't do so because it was copyrighted material that required written authorization from the publisher.

The customer continued to demand that the material be copied, anger rising in his voice. The employee continued to cite the copyright policy. It was clear to me that the customer was not going to get the employee to budge. The situation was *take it or leave it*, and the customer acted as though his arguing would get the employee to give up the need to be right. The customer stormed out of the store and, I'm sure, immediately called a friend to complain about the "lousy service" (remember: we never really avoid conflict, we simply complain about it to anyone who will listen).

Many of us are like this customer, thinking that if we just keep arguing long enough the other person will eventually give in. This does happen occasionally, which is why some people continue to argue—even in *take it or leave it* circumstances.

In *take it or leave it* situations, you have only two choices: take it . . . or leave it. In these circumstances, the person who has the power will win. "Power" may be determined by position in an organization, by the existence of a policy or procedure, or—in a family—by who can scream the loudest or pout the longest.

If you are in a power position, you can always get your way because, ultimately, you can fire the other person (divorce might be the corollary in a marriage).

There are, however, possible negative consequences attendant upon using your power in this way. At work, the consequence may be that the person will stay in her job and subtly undermine your every decision. In a family, a teenager who feels backed into a corner can make your life miserable.

So I recommend that positional power (which provides the basis for *take it or leave it* ultimatums) be used sparingly. However, it's important to recognize that there are times when you simply must be "right." In those situations, don't worry about giving up the need to be right. You are right . . . at least for those circumstances and in those situations.

If you do present a *take it or leave it* ultimatum, be prepared for the kind of anger and resentment that the copy store employee encountered. After all, the other person is being asked to take it ("give up the need to be right") or leave it (be forced to give up getting you to change), You should always listen with understanding (pay special attention to Chapter 10,) but do not change your position. If you change your position, you will undermine your power and, as noted above, make it that much harder to use your power the next time.

Of course, it's possible to see yourself as "right" even when the situation isn't all that clear. It's important to continually challenge yourself about whether your use of power is appropriate or simply your frustrated reaction to your inability to resolve the conflict. If it's the latter, consider that your inability to resolve the situation may result from the fact that you won't give up the need to be right about some aspect of the issue.

If you are on the receiving end of a *take it or leave i*, test the strength of the position before taking it or leaving it. Some people present positions as though they are *take it or leave it* when in fact it is only a negotiating tactic (and some people are simply the proverbial "bull in a china shop" and present everything in this manner). Skilled negotiators know that, in general, those who ask for more get more and have learned to pretend that their position is *take it or leave it* when, in truth, it is not.

Therefore, ask the other person, "Are you open to talking about this?" when you are presented with a *take it or leave it* ultimatum. Chapters 8-14 will show you the steps to follow if the other person is open to having a conversation.

Coaching Tips From Chapter 3:

1. Take it or leave is an ultimatum and is not open to the "Everyone Wins" model of conflict resolution.

2. Use 'take it or leave it' sparingly. No one likes to be backed into a corner.

3. Be sure that 'take it or leave it' is appropriate and not simply a reaction to your frustration.

4. Test the strength of 'take it or leave it' positions when they are used on you.

CHAPTER 3 ASSIGNMENTS

Use the space below (or your private journal) to do the following:

1. Review the names of the people with whom you are in an unresolved conflict. For each person, ask yourself whether you need his or her *commitment* or only his or her *compliance*. Circle or underline the condition in the space beneath each name. (**Caution:** *do not circle "compliance" simply because you want to avoid the conflict*).

2. Conversely, notice if all the other person needs from you is your compliance. Circle or underline "Self" if you need to commit or comply with the other person. Circle or underline "Other" if the other person needs to commit or comply with you.

3. Set a date (**put it in your calendar!**) when you will request that the other person comply, or set a date when you will comply to the other person's request (remember, however, that this most emphatically does not mean that you are giving up getting your needs met. What this may mean, however, is that you're giving up getting your needs met from that person).

Name:	
Commit / Comply	Self / Other When?
Name:	
Commit / Comply	Self / Other When?
Name:	
Commit / Comply	Self / Other When?
Name:	
Commit / Comply	Self / Other When?
Name:	
Commit / Comply	Self / Other When?

Optional assignment: Write down your thoughts and feelings about your conflicts. You may choose to use the space below or to create a separate journal.

Remember: As your coach, I'm not asking you to agree with me. I am asking you to temporarily put aside your judgments and opinions and simply do the assignments.

TODAY'S DATE: _____

Thoughts and Feelings:

_____
_____
_____
_____
_____
_____
_____
_____
_____
_____
_____
_____
_____
_____
_____
_____
_____
_____
_____
_____
_____
_____
_____
_____

You Can't Always Get What You Want, But You Can Always Get What You Need

will always be grateful to the Rolling Stones and their song "What You Want" as the inspiration for this chapter title.

More than a year after he had attended a seminar taught by Michael Nees and me, a participant called to compliment us on what he had learned. He told us that he "never gets stuck" when in a conflict. He said that he is always able to come to an agreement.

And what was the key piece of learning that was allowing him to do this for over a year? He told us that he learned the difference between wants and needs and he took to heart a key element of this distinction: **people will argue over wants but they will negotiate over needs.**

Assuming that you've given up your need to be right and that the situation you're facing is not an ultimatum (*take it or leave it*), **conflict resolution is easy: Find out what people *need***

and . . . give it to them or help them to get it. After all, "Everyone Wins" if everyone's needs are met.

Of course, giving people what they need is not always possible. You may have to say "no" to the other person once you find out her need, or you may not be able to help her once you do find out. However, the process remains the same; find out what the other person needs and give it to her, or help her get it if you can.

So what is a need and how is it distinguished from a want?

Simply put, a "want" is anything perceived as being:

- In short supply;
- A limited resource; or
- Difficult to get.

Typical "wants" are time, money and/or people.

In the world of wants, there will usually be a winner and a loser, with the "loser" being the one who gets, for example, less money, fewer people and/or has to produce results in a limited time frame. In a world of limited resources, there are often arguments over how those resources are to be allocated.

In this world, the person who has the "power" (usually due to authority) will get what he wants and the others will be left with whatever is left over. It's a prescription for dissatisfaction and conflict.

Consider a common example: During the budgeting process in a company, there is, typically, a conflict over how much money to give to each department. Since money is a limited resource, one department will inevitably receive more money than another. Arguments often ensue over how these dollars should be divided.

The situation is not dissimilar in a family. Suppose you and your spouse have one car (a "limited resource") and both of you have to get somewhere at the same time. Whoever doesn't get the car, must find alternate transportation and thus has "lost."

The world of *needs*, on the other hand, is a world of *unlimited possibilities*. People will negotiate over needs because there is the perception that there are multiple ways to meet needs, so one doesn't have to be attached to getting only what one wants.

You can move from the world of wants to the world of needs by asking the question "Why is that important to you?"

For example, assume you're involved in the budgeting process described above. Stanley, from the operations department, is making the case that his department should get more money than your department. Money, of course, is the limited resource over which there might be an argument. Stanley maintains that his department needs the additional funds to complete the creation and installation of the company web site, to hire another customer service person, and to provide training for the field sales representatives.

When Stanley is done speaking, you ask him, "Why is it important for your department to complete that installation, hire a customer service person and train the field sales reps?"

Stanley says, "Well" (with an implied "you dummy"), "the web site will **increase sales**, the customer service person will **ensure our customer's questions are answered promptly** and the training will give our sales reps the **tools to close more sales.**"

I've boldfaced the needs in each one of those responses. I suggest that, with some creative brainstorming (Chapter 13), you may find several ways by which sales might be increased (without a web site), customer's questions answered (without hiring a customer service person) and more sales closed (without more training).

I'm not suggesting that you refuse to consider web site installation, the customer service person, or the training. I'm simply using this as a demonstration of how, even when it appears as though no resolution is possible, a conflict can be moved forward simply by shifting the conversation from wants to needs.

You could spend a long time arguing over who is more deserving of the money. These arguments often end with the decision being made by someone higher in authority. You might, instead, negotiate over getting everyone's needs met. These negotiations are more likely to conclude with both sides feeling as though "Everyone Wins."

Or go back to the earlier scenario in which you and your spouse have only one car and both of you must get somewhere at the same time. Obviously, while both of you may **want** the car, neither of you **needs** the car. What do you need?

Again, ask the question that will uncover the need: "Why is having the car important to you?" The answer is obvious: "To get where I need to go." While you may only have one car and might argue for a long time over who should get it, neither one of you needs the car. What you both need is "to get where I need to go" and there are several ways to meet that need—a cab for one of you, public transportation for one or both of you, or maybe even one driving the other and being willing to do a pickup later on the person dropped off.

This simple example shows the power of distinguishing wants from needs. You and your spouse may argue for a long time over who has the "right" to the car with the person who doesn't get the car feeling angry and upset. You might, instead, negotiate over how both of you can get to where you need to go. That negotiation might very well end with a kiss.

Here's another example, this one from my life.

As I noted earlier, I live in Phoenix. I flew into Chicago's O'Hare airport for a meeting, and my friend Ron had promised to pick me up.

I had asked Ron to turn on his cell phone so that I could call him in case we had difficulty finding each other. This had long been a bone of contention between us. Ron would rarely turn on his cell phone, and I would continually request that he do so. To me, he seemed resistant to doing what I thought of as an obvious and simple request.

As I waited for Ron by the curb at the airport, I called his house to see if he had yet left to pick me up. He lived about 25 minutes away. His wife, Pam, answered and told me that he had left 15 minutes earlier.

I asked her if Ron had turned on his cell phone. She laughed. "Of course not," she said. She and I had talked in the past about this (as I noted earlier, you can never really avoid conflict; if we can't resolve an issue with someone, we often talk about that person behind his back).

"Why does he do that?" I asked and then quickly added, "I guess he just wants to be right about it."

Let's pause here a moment. Do you see my blind spot? Of course you do. It's always easy to see someone else's blind spot. But we may need a coach or really honest friend to help us see ours.

It took me a few minutes, but I eventually did see my blind spot, too. I had to laugh at my arrogance. In that moment, it became clear to me who was keeping this trivial cell phone issue going . . . and it wasn't Ron. *I* was the person who had to be right and I was the person who had to have his way. Ron was perfectly fine with not turning on his cell phone. I was the upset one, and I was the one who had to be right.

I *wanted* Ron to pick me up at the airport. However, once I gave up my need to be right, I saw that I didn't *need* him to pick me up. I asked myself, "Why is it important for him to turn on his cell phone?" The answer came back, "So that we can find each other."

The next obvious question was "Why is it important that we find each other?" and the obvious answer was "So that I can get to my meeting."

I'm sure you can see that there were multiple ways for me to get to my meeting, none of which involved Ron and his cell phone. I could choose to argue with Ron over his cell phone or I could give up the need to be right and find ways to get my needs met.

As before, I'm not suggesting that I should give up getting what I want. Certainly, the most expedient way for me to get to my meeting would have been for Ron and me to find each other (which, by the way, we did). I'm simply using this as an example of how giving up the need to be right opens up the possibility of getting our needs met.

The same process applies when dealing with your boss or someone who is higher up in the organization than you are.

Your boss, of course, can demand (*take it or leave it*) that you do what she wants, because she has more power than you. As noted in the last chapter, though, you may first want to test whether your boss is indeed delivering an ultimatum.

Here's an example of how that conversation might proceed:

You: I **want** to promote Joe to that open supervisor position in the customer service department.

Boss: You've got to be kidding. Joe doesn't have the leadership capabilities necessary for that kind of responsibility.

You (testing take it or leave it): Are you saying there are no conditions under which you'd consider a promotion for Joe?

Boss: Not exactly. It's just that I don't think Joe is ready to take the job.

You: Well, what do you think Joe is lacking?

Boss: It's clear to me that he's just not assertive enough.

You: Why is it important that he be assertive?

Boss: He's going to have to face the hard customer issues that the customer service reps can't handle. That's going to require a toughness that Joe just doesn't have.

In this instance, the boss wasn't issuing an ultimatum. He simply had a need that wasn't being met. While the boss *wants* to prevent Joe from being promoted (while you want to promote him), what he really *needs* is proof that Joe has the necessary assertiveness to handle tough customers You may argue with your boss for a long time over whether Joe should be promoted (and the boss will win if she chooses), but there may be multiple ways to prove Joe's assertiveness.

Alternatively, if the boss is adamant (*take it or leave it*), that Joe not be promoted to the open position, then you must be willing to leave it. You may not get what you want from you boss, but you can always get what you need.

Simply ask yourself, "Why is it important to me for Joe to be promoted?" Perhaps the issue isn't Joe's promotion at all. Perhaps you simply *want* to promote Joe as a way to meet your *need* to reward a good employee. There are many ways to reward an employee (your need) without necessarily promoting him (your want).

As you're distinguishing wants from needs, remember that *the one need you must be willing to relinquish* is your need to be right. In the budgeting example, you must be open to the possibility that the other person is right and should be given the money he requests. In the car example, you must be open to the possibility that your spouse is right and has a greater claim to the car than you do. In the job promotion example, you must be open to the possibility that your boss is right and Joe shouldn't be promoted.

So, whenever you encounter resistance, be sure to remember to ask the key question—"Why is that important to you?"—in order to uncover the needs(s).

COACHING TIPS FROM CHAPTER 4:

1. People will argue over wants and negotiate over needs.

2. Conflict resolution is easy: find out what people need and, if you can, give it to them.

3. The world of wants is one of limited resources while the world of needs is one of unlimited possibilities.

4. Asking the question *"Why is that important to you?"* will uncover the needs.

5. If you want to resolve a conflict so that "Everyone Wins", the one need you must be willing to give up is the need to be right.

CHAPTER 4 ASSIGNMENTS

Use the space below (or your private journal) to do the following:

1. Review the names of the people with whom you are in an unresolved conflict.

2. Beside each name, write down what **each person has said he wants.**

3. Beneath each name, write down what **you want.**

4. For each want (yours and theirs), ask the question "Why is it important for them (and you) to get those wants?" Write down whatever answers come to you. Using a separate piece of paper, write the headings as shown below.

In Chapter 10 you'll see how listening to others is the only sure way to determine what others want and need. However, it's useful to go into a conflict resolution discussion with some sense of what other's needs are so that you can plan for how you might meet those needs as well as your own.

Name:	Wants:
What I want:	
Why are the needs of each of us important in this case?	
My Needs Are Important Because:	
The Other Person's Needs Are Important Because:	

Optional assignment: Write down your thoughts and feelings about your conflicts. You may choose to use the space below or to create a separate journal.

Remember: As your coach, I'm not asking you to agree with me. I am asking you to temporarily put aside your judgments and opinions and simply do the assignments.

TODAY'S DATE: _____

Thoughts and Feelings:

_____

_____

_____

_____

_____

_____

_____

_____

_____

_____

_____

_____

_____

_____

_____

_____

_____

_____

To Play Or To Pass:
That is the Question

You've completed your warm-ups. You've stretched your thinking, and perhaps you just can't wait to begin playing the game.

But before you begin to expend your time and energy, there are two choices you must make. This chapter discusses whether you should choose to play the game at all; the next chapter will help you analyze whom you should be playing with.

The chart on the next page shows the process you will now follow as you create an **Everyone Wins** solution to your conflicts. Our consulting firm's Managing Partner, Michael Nees, created the chart.

Play or Pass? → Pass

Opening Moves

Conflict

Choose to consider other perspectives

1. Listen!

Repeat this cycle
until mutual,
respectful understanding
of underlying needs
and wants emerges
and common ground
is discovered

2. Bridge

Choose to seek *Everyone Wins!* solution

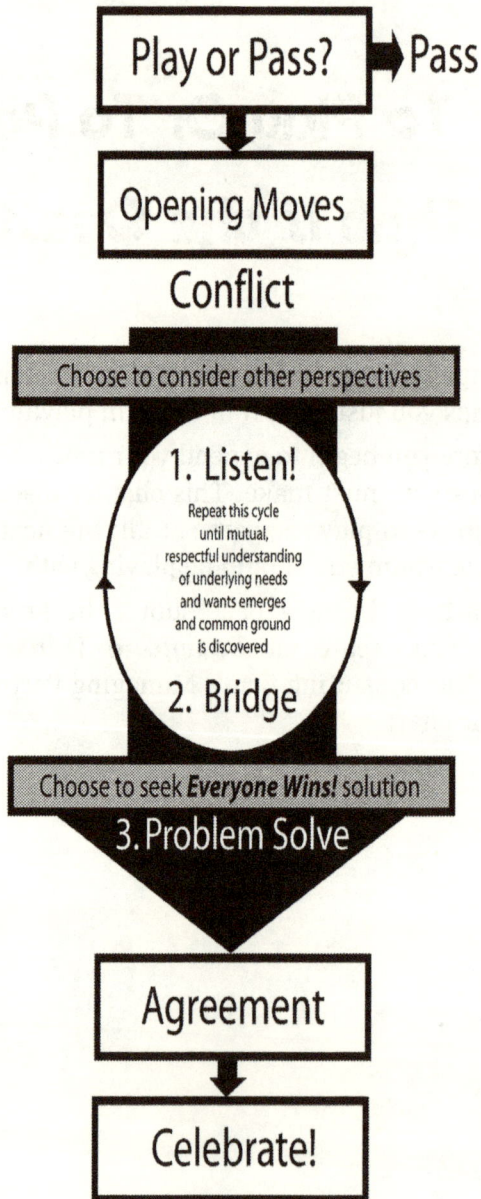

3. Problem Solve

Agreement

Celebrate!

Here are examples of situations where you'd have to make the choice to play or pass:

- The boss wants you to take on a new project, even though you're already swamped. On the one hand, you want to confront your boss about taking on a new assignment; on the other hand, you don't want to appear difficult because you fear that any difficulty you cause or can be blamed for could affect your career negatively. Should you confront your boss (play) or just take on the new project and say nothing (pass)?

- A co-worker has been late getting his portion of a report to you. The final report is due in only two days, and you'll have to work extra long hours to complete your portion and meet the deadline. This is the second time this has happened. You want to confront the co-worker and get his commitment to complete his work on a timely basis (play), but you don't want to take up even more time having that discussion. It seems easier to say nothing and just work harder when you need to (pass).

- A friend you're having lunch with is expressing strong views about his support for what's happening in some political situation. You don't agree. You want to stand up for what you believe, but you don't want to get into a seemingly endless and fruitless debate. Should you express your disagreement openly (play) or should you choose to say nothing (pass)?

- Your spouse wants a new dishwasher, but you'd like to delay the purchase until you feel more comfortable spending the money. Getting into conflict with your spouse might disturb the domestic tranquility, but you don't want to break the family bank. Should you talk to your spouse about your misgivings (play) or should you say nothing and purchase the dishwasher (pass)?

In every one of these scenarios and the hundreds more you may encounter during the course of a week, you need to make a choice: Do I state my opinion and express my disagreement ("play"), or do I avoid doing so at this time and perhaps forever ("Pass").

And that leads to a distinction between "at this time" and "forever."

We saw in Chapter 1 that conflict can never be completely avoided. It may be avoided between you and others, but it will come out in the conversations you have with them, or simply in the discomfort you experience whenever you think about or come into contact with that person. That's why, even if you avoid the conflict "at this time", I recommend that, at some point in the very near future you confront the disagreement directly and use what you learn in this book to resolve it, if for no other reason than to preserve your own peace of mind.

However, in spite of what I just wrote, you may choose to avoid conflict anyway. If you make this choice, you must completely and **forever** give up your need to be right. As you know, there are situations which you decide just aren't worth your time and energy. Political debates may fall into this category. Whether to go to a movie or to go bowling may fall into this category. Whether your name or your partner's name should go first on the new brochure may fall into this category. *Take it or leave it* situations can be included here, too. Choosing to avoid conflict doesn't mean you agree with the other person. You will still have your opinion. You are simply choosing to let the other person "win" this time by keeping your disagreements to yourself.

If you choose to pass in a conflict, you must agree to never (as in **never**) complain or boast to anyone (and I mean **anyone**) about your choice to let the other person "win". In fact, you must forever give up even talking about the conflict to anyone at all (including those you are closest to).

Blaming others is a sure sign that passing the conflict is not working for you, and such behavior on your part indicates you must play the game of conflict with the person whom you are complaining about. As a corollary, boasting to others about your decision not to play the game is an empty way of still being "right." If you find this happening, you probably need to deal with the conflict right away; otherwise, it will keep eating away at you and you will keep boasting—or maybe return to complaining. None of it works!

Suppose, however, that you find that you simply cannot let go of the disagreement, but it is still not worth your energy to engage with the other person. In that case, you must find another way to get your needs met.

Remember the question to ask to determine your needs: *"Why is getting this important to me?"* Why is having your name first on the brochure important to you? Why is going to a movie versus bowling important to you? Why is it so important that the other person see the validity of your political position? Your answers will give you access to your true needs, and you must find a way to get those needs met or you will continue to be dissatisfied.

The choice to play or pass is one we make many times every day, either consciously or unconsciously. Some instances are so minor that it's easy to choose to pass them (did that person intentionally jump in line ahead of you or was it an oversight? Oh, well, it will only be an extra minute or two . . .), and some are not so easy to pass (if I take on that extra project from my boss, I may disappoint my co-workers and delay even further the project we're working on).

Sometimes we pass conflict when there are, in truth, good reasons for doing so (do you really want to argue over where you're going to eat lunch?). However, some of us pass conflict habitually and then wonder why we're upset so much of the time.

Let's face it: if you pass conflict and don't get your needs met on a regular basis, you're going to be upset. In fact, as noted in Chapter 2, many people who habitually pass conflict end up blaming the other person for being "argumentative" rather than taking personal responsibility for their avoidance.

COACHING TIPS FROM CHAPTER 5:

1. You must choose to either play the game of conflict (it's worth your time and energy to do so) or to pass on the conflict (it's not worth your time and energy to do so).

2. If you choose not to play, you must choose to pass temporarily (you will engage in the near future) or permanently (you will never complain).

3. Blaming others is a sure sign that passing the conflict isn't working for you.

CHAPTER 5 ASSIGNMENTS

Use the space below (or your private journal) to do the following:

1. Review the names of the people with whom you're in an unresolved conflict.

2. Choose whether to play or pass by writing the word "play" or "pass" beside each name.

3. For those people with whom you are choosing to pass conflict, choose whether this is permanent or temporary.

4. If temporary, set a date when you will engage in the conflict with this person.

5. If permanent, completely give up your need to be right and find alternative ways to meet your needs.

Name	Play/Pass?	Perm/Temp	When?

Optional assignment: Write down your thoughts and feelings about your conflicts. You may choose to use the space below or to create a separate journal.

Remember: As your coach, I'm not asking you to agree with me. I am asking you to temporarily put aside your judgments and opinions and simply do the assignments.

TODAY'S DATE: _____

Thoughts and Feelings:

_____

_____

_____

_____

_____

_____

_____

_____

_____

_____

_____

_____

_____

_____

_____

_____

_____

_____

_____

_____

_____

_____

Chapter 6

With Whom Should I Play The Game?

The rule here is very simple: If at all possible, engage only with the person who has the power to institute the change you're looking for. To determine who this is, ask yourself, *"Who is the decision maker in this situation?"*

For example, I was coaching a woman (Joan) who was a Vice President of Regulatory Affairs. Joan was responsible for making sure that the company's products were manufactured using standards established by the government. The meaning of the standards wasn't always clear and part of her job was to figure out how to interpret the standards when there was a lack of clarity.

She was in current conflict with a peer (Steve) over the interpretation of one of these standards. Joan was reluctant to confront Steve directly, because she had had conflicts with him in the past and had been unable to resolve them satisfactorily. Because of this history, Joan had sometimes gone to Steve's boss to enlist his assistance in getting Steve to change. Steve had resented Joan for going around him in the past, and this mind-set caused Steve to resent Joan all the more in the current situation.

I coached Joan to go to Steve directly even though she felt uncomfortable doing so. Because an attitudinal change was needed, Steve was the only person who could actually make that change (the "decision maker"), and as I said to Joan, this could turn out to be a way to strengthen the relationship with Steve.

Here's another typical situation. Let's say you have a weekly meeting scheduled with a co-worker who consistently calls up at the last minute to say she'll be late meeting you. You find yourself complaining about her to others, but you know that such talk will make absolutely no difference in her behavior. In fact, if your co-worker hears about the gossip, it will only harm the relationship. Only by confronting your co-worker directly will you have the chance to both resolve the issue and strengthen the relationship. Additionally, your co-worker is ultimately the "decision maker" in this case, the only person who can choose to come to the meetings on time.

Gossip is severely dis-empowering because it keeps you from actually confronting the person with whom you have the issue. While it can sometimes seem cathartic to gossip, it's much more likely to leave you even more frustrated because it does nothing to resolve the conflict.

At the beginning of this Chapter, I wrote that you should play the game of conflict only with the person who has the power to make the change you want **if at all possible.** There are, of course, times when you can't directly confront the decision maker because other people are between you and that person.

For example, James, a sales representative, wanted his company to change the pricing structure on a particular product line. The Vice President of Sales and Marketing could make that decision, but James' boss was the Director of Sales, not the Vice President. It would have been inappropriate for James to go directly to the Vice President of Sales and Marketing. James had to first convince his immediate boss that the price change was the right thing to do. Only then could he hope to go to the Vice President. James used the *Everyone Wins* process to convince his boss of the value of changing the pricing, and when the time came to make the case to the decision maker, James and his boss approached the Vice President together—a much stronger and more credible case was the result, and James got his price increase.

Sometimes, there is more than one decision maker. For example, in many businesses, a committee makes decisions. And every one of us I'm sure remembers asking our mothers if we could do something, only to be told to "go ask your father."

In a business where the committee system is in effect, there are usually one or perhaps two people on the committee to whom the committee defers. Find out who these people are and what they need, respond to those needs and you can, often, convince the committee.

COACHING TIPS FROM CHAPTER 6:

1. **If at all possible, play the game only with the person who has the power to make the change you want.**

2. **Determine who has the power by asking, "Who is the decision maker in this situation?"**

3. **Even in situations where there are multiple decision makers, there are usually one or two people who control the decision. Find out who these people are and what they need.**

ASSIGNMENT FROM CHAPTER 6

Use the space below (or your private journal) to do the following:
1. Review the names of the people with whom you are in an unresolved conflict.
2. For each person, ask if this is the person who has the power to institute the change you want (the "decision maker").
3. If it is not the appropriate person, write down the name of the person who does have the power (remember, however, that you might have to first enlist this person before going to the person who does have the power).

Name:	Decision maker?	Y	N
If not, then who?			
Name:	Decision maker?	Y	N
If not, then who?			
Name:	Decision maker?	Y	N
If not, then who?			
Name:	Decision maker?	Y	N
If not, then who?			
Name:	Decision maker?	Y	N
If not, then who?			

Optional assignment: Write down your thoughts and feelings about your conflicts. You may choose to use the space below or to create a separate journal.

Remember: As your coach, I'm not asking you to agree with me. I am asking you to temporarily put aside your judgments and opinions and simply do the assignments.

TODAY'S DATE: _____

Thoughts and Feelings:

_____

_____

_____

_____

_____

_____

_____

_____

_____

_____

_____

_____

_____

_____

_____

_____

_____

_____

_____

_____

_____

Chapter 7

Time Out: Plan to Celebrate Everyone Winning the Game

Enough with the warm-ups. You're about to begin playing the game. I offer this "time out" for you to catch your breath, relax and visualize the end of the game even before you begin playing.

The runner about to run a race in the Olympics visualizes himself breaking the tape at the end as he crosses the finish line ahead of the other runners. He sees himself exalt in the victory. He imagines the accolades of the crowd. He sees himself on the victory stand and hears the band play his country's National anthem while the crowd sings along. In his mind, the effort he is about to expend will be worth it in order to arrive at this moment of achievement and celebration.

So, too, as you are about to "run your race", I encourage you to plan for the celebration at the end. If you use what you will learn in this book to resolve your conflicts, you will arrive at a moment of achievement and celebration. Plan for the reward you will give yourself in order to motivate yourself to go through the steps in the following chapters. Like the runner, you want to know that the effort you're about to expend to resolve your conflicts will have been worth it.

Imagine how you'll feel when a key conflict is resolved. Imagine the smiles on your face and the faces of the others involved when you realize that at last your needs and the needs of others involved have been met and you can put this issue behind you. Feel the sense of happiness and release, knowing that something that has been troubling you is no longer a concern. Hear the words as you congratulate yourself and the person with whom you've been in conflict. You've persevered in spite of the obstacles in your way.

The only difference between the runner and you is that the runner will stand alone on the winner's platform while your victory will be shared with those with whom you've been in conflict.

Think of significant events in your life—like your birthday, the day you got the job you've always wanted, the birthdays of your children or your wedding anniversary. Certainly, you highlighted the event with some minor or major celebration—a card, a dinner, a party, a cigar, champagne, a vacation, a special purchase. Isn't the resolution of a conflict a significant event? Shouldn't it be celebrated as well?

You may think it's strange to plan to celebrate an event whose outcome is still in doubt. Suppose you get to the finish line and not everyone has won? What will there be to celebrate?

My answer is that if you get to the "finish line" and not everyone has won, you're not at the finish line. As I've noted several times, the "finish line" is when everyone's needs have been met. Keep going until that happens. Your celebration will mark that moment.

In Chapter 15, I'll return to this topic and ask you to execute your plan. In addition to celebrating then, I encourage you to celebrate NOW. We usually celebrate only when major milestones have been reached—when a conflict is resolved, when a project is completed, when a purchase order is signed, when we are promoted, on a birthday or anniversary, and so forth. However, it's hard to maintain passion and excitement if that milestone is far in the future, as it might be if you're dealing with a long-standing conflict.

Therefore: Put this book down and celebrate RIGHT NOW! Go to a movie. Have a great meal. Eat a terrific dessert (someone shared with me that "stressed" is simply "desserts" spelled backwards). Shop for new clothes. Do something that you have been looking forward to doing.

You may be wondering what there is to celebrate right now. I suggest you celebrate that you've come this far, that you've put aside your judgments and opinions, and that you've accepted the coaching this book has offered you so far. If nothing else, celebrate the knowledge that in order to have arrived at this point you've finally given up your need to be right.

Since I'm not there to express my gratitude and to congratulate you, my coaching is that you find a way **right now** to congratulate yourself.

COACHING TIP FROM CHAPTER 7:

It's important to celebrate to keep yourself motivated as you work through conflict.

ASSIGNMENT FROM CHAPTER 7

Do the following—right here and right now!

1. Put this book down RIGHT NOW and celebrate your achievements (perhaps it's only to get up to dance and sing or to eat a cupcake before you start reading again).

2. Use the space below to plan for how you will celebrate on the day you resolve your biggest conflict—on that big day when "Everyone Wins."

_____
_____
_____
_____
_____
_____
_____
_____
_____
_____
_____
_____
_____
_____
_____
_____
_____
_____
_____
_____
_____

Optional assignment: Write down your thoughts and feelings about your conflicts. You may choose to use the space below or to create a separate journal.

Remember: As your coach, I'm not asking you to agree with me. I am asking you to temporarily put aside your judgments and opinions and simply do the assignments.

TODAY'S DATE: _____

Thoughts and Feelings:

_____

_____

_____

_____

_____

_____

_____

_____

_____

_____

_____

_____

_____

_____

_____

_____

_____

_____

_____

_____

_____

PART 2:

LET THE GAMES BEGIN

Chapter 8

Step 1:

The Opening Moves

A race begins when the starter's gun is fired. A baseball game begins when the umpire shouts, "Play ball." A football game begins when the referee blows his whistle.

A conflict begins when one person either attempts to persuade another ("We should do it for these reasons . . . ") or attempts to inspire another ("Can you imagine if . . . ") or makes a request of another ("I Want . . . ")—and that other person disagrees.

If someone attempts to influence you to change and you disagree with what you're being requested to do, skip to Chapter 10, "Listening: The Judo of the 'Everyone Wins' Game", to understand how to proceed.

However, if you are the one attempting to influence someone else to change, the game begins with one of three options. Since the way you begin often dictates how well the game will be played, choose your opening moves carefully.

The three options for your opening moves are:

Persuasion, Inspiration and Assertion.

Option 1: Persuasion

Persuasion involves making a suggestion and providing reasons why that suggestion should be adopted. Particularly in

Western cultures, this is the most common way to attempt to influence others. There is a general belief that the most logical argument is the one that prevails.

Your own experience has probably taught you the fallacy of this notion. I'm sure you've had the experience of knowing that your logic is completely unassailable and being astounded when others don't immediately agree with you and act accordingly.

The most important thing to know about *persuasion* is that **you must limit the number of reasons you offer for why others should agree with you.** In fact, **the more reasons you use in support of your argument, the weaker your argument.**

Have you ever considered buying something and had the salesperson keep giving you reasons for buying long after you've obviously already made up your mind to buy or not to buy? What is your reaction when this occurs?

If you have already made up your mind to buy but the sales person keeps selling, you may begin to question the "rightness" of your purchasing decision. After all, if the product or service is so good, why does the salesperson feel compelled to keep giving you reasons for buying?

And if you've made up your mind not to buy but the salesperson keeps selling, you've probably become annoyed and even stopped listening.

The same thing can occur when *you* use persuasion. You may have ten reasons why someone should do as you ask. And they all may be good and valid points. But wait. Select your two strongest reasons and present only those. If your two strongest reasons don't move the other person, what makes you think eight more reasons will?

It's like the person who goes to visit a friend and knocks on the door. No answer. So he knocks a little louder. Still no answer. He then knocks even more forcefully. Still no answer. Finally, in frustration, the visitor kicks the door and still there is no answer.

What advice would you give to this frustrated person? You'd probably counsel him to stop knocking. No one is home.

The same is true with your persuasive arguments. "Stop knocking" if the other person isn't moved by them. In this book, "stop knocking" means "start listening" which we'll explore in much more depth in Chapter 10. In case you're wondering "What about my other eight wonderful arguments?", we will see later that there will be plenty of time to bring up the other persuasive points in your arsenal—the key to when and how will be revealed through your listening skills

Persuasion works best when emotions are muted and people are open to logic and reasoning. For example, I once facilitated a conflict between representatives from the Sales Department and the Production Department of the same company. Production was upset that Sales was making promises to customers without first checking to see if Production could actually fulfill on those promises. Sales was upset, believing that Production just wasn't working hard enough (or smart enough).

The Production representatives brought their work schedules and manufacturing flow charts to the meeting and were able to demonstrate to Sales that, in fact,

- The plant was running at full capacity
- Production was rejecting very few parts, and
- They were making effective use of the available labor; therefore,
- The promises that salespeople were making to customers just couldn't be fulfilled.

Even though the people in the Sales Department had been upset, they were willing to put that emotion aside after seeing the schedules and hearing the Production Department's reasoning. After some quibbling (no one easily gives up the need to be right), Sales eventually agreed and started making more realistic promises to customers.

It's rather simple to determine if your persuasive argument is having the desired effect. After you have presented your two or three strongest reasons why the other person should agree with you, ask, "What do you think?" If the other person agrees with you, persuasion has been effective. If the other person doesn't agree with you, your attempt at persuasion has been ineffective so far, and you must move to "listening" (Chapter 10) to find out why you have not been persuasive.

Option 2: Inspiration

Were you alive in 1963? If you were, I'm sure you've heard or read or seen Martin Luther King's "I Have A Dream" speech, the famous one that was delivered on the steps of the Lincoln Memorial in Washington, D.C. during a march for civil rights. If you weren't alive, I'm still sure you at least know of the speech. Dr. King has been dead for many years, yet his message continues to inspire us with its vision of possibility for humanity.

That is the power of *inspiration*. Using persuasion to influence others may not work because there may not be logical reasons for someone to change. But if you can connect with another's heart, you can often move him or her to change. Some people are even moved to tears when we are able to connect with *their* ideals and aspirations.

You may be thinking, ". . . But I'm not an inspirational person." I remember hearing this often when I suggested to a group of engineers that they attempt to influence others using inspiration rather than persuasion. However, when I pressed them to try, they surprised themselves with how effective they were.

Perhaps, like those engineers, you've spent so long using persuasion that you've come to believe it's the only approach you're really good at. If so, I encourage you to do what you must always do to prove to yourself that you can master a skill: practice, practice, and practice some more, using inspiration to influence people to change.

The persuasive argument that sounds like "We should adopt this proposal for the following three reasons" could also be presented inspirationally, like this: "Can you see the smiling faces of our customers, hear the delight in their voices, and feel your deep satisfaction for a job well done, when the shipment arrives on time and ahead of schedule?"

The persuasive argument "Our company values will give us a competitive advantage because . . ." could also be stated inspirationally as: "Having the integrity to keep our promises, the discipline to persevere in the face of obstacles, and the courage to say yes when we yearn to say no will make us better suppliers for our customers and better people for our families."

The persuasive argument "We need to operate as a team because . . ." might be transformed into "An individual voice has power, but not the power of a choir. An individual oarsman has speed, but not the speed of a crew. A man alone can move heavy boulders, but men together can move mountains."

It takes longer to create an inspirational statement than a persuasive one (at least it does for me), but the impact can be far more memorable and survive longer in the mind of the listener.

An inspirational appeal can move people to take action even in the face of uncertainty and fear. Of course, once people are inspired to take action, there must be a logical plan for how to proceed. Inspiration engages the heart, but the head must also be attached. Inspiration without a plan is like clapping with one hand (possible only for very advanced Zen Buddhists, I am told).

Just as with a persuasive appeal, end your inspirational appeal with "What do you think?" If you get agreement, inspiration has been successful. If you don't get agreement, using inspiration has not been successful, and as noted earlier, you must move to "listening" (Chapter 10) to find out why you have not been successful. It's just that simple.

Option 3: Assertion

I learned long ago that many people don't get what they want (or need) because they don't clearly ask for it. *Assertion* assures clarity about what you want or need. It's absolutely clear what a person wants when he says, "I want you to be here on time" or "I want you to read the manual before asking questions" or "I want you to take the dog to the vet".

Persuasion includes reasons and appeals to logic. Inspiration does not include reasons and appeals to the emotions. Assertion simply states what you want. You want it because you want it. In fact, you might say that, when you are asserting, you are being unreasonable. Don't add any reasons to your assertion and use as few words as possible. The more words you use, the weaker your assertion. For example:

- **"I want you to be here on time"** may become "I know it's difficult for you, but I really need you to be here on time." When you "assert" in this way, you signal to the other person that it really is difficult to be on time and that, perhaps if he has a good excuse, you might forgive him.

- **"I want you to read the manual before asking questions"** may become "I know that's a lot of reading and it's not the most interesting reading, but it's important that you familiarize yourself with this material so I'd like you to read it." The person you're addressing may interpret your statement to mean "I'd like you to familiarize yourself with this material" and only skim through the manual. After all, "it's not the most interesting reading."

- **"I want you to pick up the dog from the vet"** may become "I know you've got a million things to do (no he doesn't, although he may have 3 or 4), but if it wouldn't be too much trouble (of course it's too much trouble from his perspective or he'd just go ahead and get the darn dog) I'd really appreciate it if you'd get the dog from the vet (Sure, you'd <u>appreciate</u> it, but how strongly do you <u>want</u> me to get the dog, dude?)."

Assertions work best in situations when:

- You want quick action;

- You want to create the impression that you have the power to force a decision; and/or

- The situation is *take it or leave it.*

You may think that using the words "I want you to..." instead of "I need you to..." or "I'd like you to..." or "if it wouldn't be too much bother" are too "pushy" or even harsh. If you think this, it may be because you believe "I want" sounds as though you're angry or upset.

This is not at all the case. In fact, because assertion is a request and not a demand, be sure that your tone of voice is pleasant and not harsh or abrasive. This may take some practice if you don't assert regularly.

For example, I was recently talking to a friend of mine who works as a consultant helping companies install large software packages for manufacturing and distribution purposes. Because big software installations rarely go smoothly, he often has to deal with customers who are sometimes upset if not outright angry. My friend would often have to assertively request that these angry people calm down so that they could listen to his proposed solutions.

He told me that if he made his request ("I want you to calm down and listen to me") using a very calm and pleasant tone, the other person invariably calmed down. If, on the other hand, he sounded angry, his experience showed that it only made the situation worse.

Some people prefer to add "please" or "I'd appreciate it" to their assertion. There's nothing wrong with either of those additions as long as you don't overdo the thanks or appreciation to the point where it sounds like begging. Be brief with both your assertion and your appreciation.

Whatever opening move you choose to use, you must check to determine if the other person is going to take action.

I recommended earlier that you end persuasive or inspirational appeals with "What do you think?". If the person responds with "That makes sense" or " I get what you're saying", and so on, then ask, "Will you do it?" "That makes sense" and "I get what you're saying" are not commitments to take action. Changing behavior is an act of will. *"Will you do it?" is a request for a commitment.*

For the same reasons, an assertive appeal should end with the question "Will you do it?"

Do not ask "Could you do it?", "Would you do it?", "Can you do it?", "Will you try and do it?", or any other such variation. The person probably could do it, would do it, can do it and will try to do it, but those are not the right questions. The only right question is, "Will you do it?"

Asking directly, assertively and uncompromisingly, does take courage, especially if the other person is your boss or someone who has more power than you do in the given situation. However, I encourage you to ask the question anyway. It will serve you well to be sure that there is a firm commitment to act.

Finally, after you ask "Will you do it?", stop talking. This is extremely important. If the other person doesn't respond immediately, the tendency may be for you to want to fill the silence. Filling the silence will give the other person the opportunity to respond to something other than your question.

COACHING TIPS FROM CHAPTER 8

Conflict begins when one person attempts to influence another using persuasion, inspiration and/or assertion — and the other person disagrees.

1. **Persuasion:**

   - Works best when emotions are muted and people are open to logic and reason
   - Involves using only your strongest reasons
   - Ends with "What do you think?" to determine if you have agreement followed by "Will you do it?"

2. **Inspiration:**

   - Works best when there is no apparent logical reason to change
   - Appeals to ideals and aspirations
   - Must be followed by a logical plan for action
   - Ends with "What do you think?" to determine if you have agreement followed by "Will you do it?"

3. **Assertion:**

   - Is "unreasonable". You want it because you want it
   - Involves using few words
   - Works best when quick action is desirable and/or you want to project power
   - Requires a pleasant tone of voice (not harsh or abrasive)
   - Ends with "Will you do it?" to determine if action will be taken

ASSIGNMENT FROM CHAPTER 8

Use the space below (or your private journal) to do the following:

1. Review the list of the people with whom you're in an unresolved conflict.

2. Put a "P" beside the person's name if you think it best to open the discussion with a persuasive approach, an "I" if you think it best to open the discussion with an inspirational approach and an "A" if you think it best to open with an assertion.

3. Experiment with different openings. For example, if you think the best approach is to use persuasion, try out an assertion

4. **On a separate piece of paper, write down the exact words** you would use to begin each of these conversations. In conflict, as in any game, the way you begin often dictates how the game will end.

5. Practice these opening moves with your "live" coach. Saying them out loud (and getting feedback) will give you a better sense of their effectiveness than simply saying them to yourself.

Name	P	I	A

Optional assignment: Write down your thoughts and feelings about your conflicts. You may choose to use the space below or to create a separate journal.

Remember: As your coach, I'm not asking you to agree with me. I am asking you to temporarily put aside your judgments and opinions and simply do the assignments.

TODAY'S DATE: _____

Thoughts and Feelings:

_____

_____

_____

_____

_____

_____

_____

_____

_____

_____

_____

_____

_____

_____

_____

_____

_____

_____

_____

_____

_____

Chapter 9

Time Out:

Express Appreciation

So you've decided to engage the other person in conflict resolution and you've presented your position using either *persuasion*, *inspiration* or *assertion*. You've asked "What do you think?" and "Will you do it?"

If the other person says "yes" in response to your question, **congratulate yourself** for being able to influence another human being to take the action you'd like her to take. But, even more importantly, you must congratulate **the other person.**

If you have been successful, you are in the presence of generosity and I don't mean *your* generosity. I'm referring to the generosity of the other person. You have just experienced a rare phenomenon. You have witnessed another human being giving up the need to be right. In order for someone to change, he has to give up his need to be right. He has been willing to listen to your perspective, and given up defending the "rightness' of his position. He has agreed with your reasons (*persuasion*) or been inspired by your appeal to his emotions (*inspiration*) or agreed to take action based on your request (*assertion*). What do you think should be your appropriate next step?

To answer that question, consider: If you were to give up the need to be right and choose to do what someone else asked you to do, what would you like to hear? Wouldn't you at the very least like to hear, "Thank you"?

And that is what you **must** do. You **must** communicate your appreciation to the other person. If you don't express some form of appreciation, he is likely to feel as though he has received nothing in return for changing and may revert to old behavior or may even sabotage the agreement to change.

A simple "thank you" is fine. It would be even better to offer some fervent expression of your recognition that he has made a huge concession. For example, "I am so grateful for your willingness to do this. I know it really takes something to make this change and I want you to know how appreciative I am."

In personal relationships, that "fervent expression" might include a hug, a pat on the back, or a kiss.

I recommend you offer appreciation even if your request for change has been *take it or leave it* (that is, the person **must** comply with your request). If the person has agreed to comply (given up his need to be right), you must acknowledge this or you will find he will be reluctant to do so again (and perhaps even resent having done it at all).

In *take it or leave it* situations, expressing appreciation can seem insincere or phony. Therefore, I suggest you express your appreciation by saying something like, "I know you really had very little choice about this, which is why I especially want to thank you."

Finally, I encourage you to find a way to express appreciation even if the conflict is still unresolved. It's easier to resolve a conflict with someone when the relationship isn't just about the conflict.

For example, you may resent your boss for dumping work on you at the last minute. You certainly don't want to thank her for contributing to your long hours at work.

However, you may really appreciate the fact that the assignments your boss does give you contain interesting problems to solve that will contribute to your career development. She's not just giving you work that she doesn't want to do herself. Thanking your boss for that will make it easier to also have the conversation about dumping work on you at the last minute.

Similarly, you many not appreciate friends who don't call you back. However, these same friends may be people you can always count on to take care of your pets when you are unexpectedly called out of town. Thanking your friends for that will make it easier to also have the conversation about not returning your calls.

COACHING TIPS FROM CHAPTER 9:

1. In order for people to change, they have to give up their need to be right.

2. Giving up the need to be right is a major concession and should be rewarded with some form of appreciation.

ASSIGNMENTS FROM CHAPTER 9

Use the space below (or your private journal) to do the following:

1. Review your list of the people with whom you're in an unresolved conflict.

2. Ask yourself: "Is there **any area** of your relationship with each person in which you could express your appreciation?

3. You may have areas of the relationship in which the person has, in fact, given up the need to be right. Or there may be areas where the person has simply done something for which you would like to thank him or her. This step is an opportunity to practice expressing appreciation in either of those circumstances.

4. Using a separate piece of paper, write down **the exact words** you would say to express your appreciation to each person.

5. Practice saying these words with your "live" coach. Saying them out loud (and getting feedback) will give you a better sense of their effectiveness than simply saying them to yourself.

Name:	Area of appreciation?

Optional assignment: Write down your thoughts and feelings about your conflicts. You may choose to use the space below or to create a separate journal.

Remember: As your coach, I'm not asking you to agree with me. I am asking you to temporarily put aside your judgments and opinions and simply do the assignments.

TODAY'S DATE: _____

Thoughts and Feelings:

_____

_____

_____

_____

_____

_____

_____

_____

_____

_____

_____

_____

_____

_____

_____

_____

_____

_____

_____

_____

_____

_____

Chapter 10

Step 2:

Listening: The "Judo"

Of the Conflict Game

*"If you listen hard enough to any person, whether they
like it or not, they will signal very clearly what they
want and what their motivations are."*

Bargaining for Advantage: Negotiation Strategies for Reasonable People
Richard Butler and G. Richard Shell

To re-cap: up to this point, you've . . .

- Presented your position (or the other person has presented hers) using either persuasion, inspiration or assertion.

- Asked "What do you think?" and "Will you do it?"

- Expressed your appreciation if the person has said, "Yes," she will do it.

But what if you get disagreement, or even a firm "No"? Let's look now at how to deal successfully with both eventualities.

A firm "No" is easily handled because it's usually *take it or leave it* and isn't amenable to the "Everyone Wins" model. Either you will do what's been requested or you will not. Either the other person will do what you've requested or she will not. This kind of "No" simply means that you will not get your needs met at this time, so you must find alternate means for doing so.

Rather than saying, "No," more often, in response to "Will you do it?" the person expresses disagreement by saying something like

- "I'm not sure I want to" or
- "That's going to be difficult" or
- "You always ask me to do things you don't want to do yourself" or
- you'll hear pseudo-agreement such as "I'll try" or "I'll do my best".

The important thing to remember is this: In response to asking, "Will you do it?" **anything but a "yes" should be heard as disagreement.** Therefore, you should hear responses in this way:

- They say, "I'm not sure I want to." You should hear, "I disagree."
- They say, "That's going to be difficult." You should hear, "I disagree."
- They say, "I'll try." You should hear, "I disagree."
- They say, "I'll do my best." You should hear, "I disagree."

I know that "I'll do my best" **sounds** like "Yes" but it's not. Only "Yes" is "yes". In reply to "I'll do my best", ask, "Does that mean you **will** do it?". You're attempting to get a clear agreement to change behavior, so you must listen very carefully to be sure you have that agreement.

In addition to listening to the words, you should also listen to the tone in which the words are said. For example, an affirmative "Yes" more likely represents a commitment than does a "Yes" said with a tentative or hesitant tone of voice.

So what do you do? If you hear anything but "Yes" in response to "Will you do it?". You listen some more. And what you're listening for is *what the person needs* because, invariably, when there is unresolved conflict, there is an un-met need.

As the Chapter title indicates, listening is the "judo" of the game of conflict. For those of you unfamiliar with judo, it is a form of self-defense in which one neutralizes one's opponent not by overcoming the opponent's strength but by using it. You can use listening in essentially the same way, only in the service of "Everyone Wins" versus the motivation of defeating an opponent.

Let me explain why this is so.

Imagine that you are standing, facing another person whose hands are together with yours, fingers interlocked, at about chest height. (To get the full impact, it would be helpful to actually do this with another person.) Now imagine that each of you uses force to attempt to move one another backwards.

What happens? If you're like the hundreds of people I've actually had do this in my workshops, what happens is . . . nothing. There is very little movement. If the two people have about equal strength, they end up in a standoff, pushing with all their might towards the other person, with neither being able to move the other very much, if at all.

Now imagine the same exercise, but this time you handle it differently. You're facing this same person, fingers interlocked and held at chest height, as before. Once again, the goal is to move the other person backward and yourself forward. This time, however, when she tries to force you backwards you offer **absolutely no resistance.** In fact, you co-operate—just a little. You relax and begin to allow her to move you backward. Then, in an instant, you use her energy by stepping sideways, swinging her around you in a half circle, so that she is now facing in the direction you were just facing and, in fact, her momentum is moving her in the direction you wanted her to go in the first place.

The other person has expended most of the energy, used most of the "force". This simple exercise provides a good analogy that demonstrates why listening is the single most valuable thing you can do when you encounter resistance.

Both of you using force in the first instance is analogous to neither one of you giving up the need to be right leading to stalemate and frustration. In fact, the next time you are in a position to observe a conflict that is not being resolved, you'll notice that this is exactly what happens. You can almost see the arguments flying back and forth from one to the other as each person tries to force the other to agree, while neither is listening very much, if at all. Often, the two people end up agreeing to disagree without resolution.

Of course, in the example of both of you using force at the same time, if one of you is physically stronger than the other, the stronger person could, in fact, force the weaker person backwards no matter how strenuously the weaker person resists. This is analogous to *take it or leave it*.

However, as you saw in Chapter 3, there are consequences to *take it or leave it*. While the stronger person may win the battle, he often loses the war. The person who has been forced to move against his will might resent it and in subtle ways sabotage the stronger person. This is why *take it or leave it* positions should be used sparingly.

Notice, on the other hand, what happened when you didn't force the other person to move but instead used her energy to move her in the direction you wanted her to move. If you really did this activity, you would have noticed how little energy had to be expended on your part, yet she ended up where you wanted her to be. Wouldn't it be great if conflicts could be resolved this easily?

Well, the fact is, they can—if you're willing to consider conflict resolution as judo and not boxing. Listening is the "judo" of conflict resolution because, when listening, you expend little energy, yet you encourage the other person to change.

Therefore, **as soon as you get disagreement, stop pushing** (i.e., give up the need to be right) and go into your "judo" mode. Start to listen to what the other person is saying to you.

How can it be that listening actually encourages the other person to change? For my scientific readers, I refer you to Newton's Third Law of Motion for confirmation of the validity of this idea. That law of physics states that for every action there is an equal and opposite reaction. For our purposes, this suggests that using force causes the other person to also use force—and listening causes the other person to listen, as well.

Consider, then, that if you're getting resistance, you're being resistant. If you're getting defensiveness, you're being defensive. If you're getting cooperation, you're being cooperative. If the other person is giving up the need to be right, so are you. *In a conflict, listening is the most valuable skill to employ, because it is how you communicate your willingness to give up the need to be right, thus encouraging the other person to give up his need to be right.*

Listening can even reduce the anger of someone who is forced into a *take it or leave it* position. No one likes to think she has no choice. But if she feels that her position has at least been heard and understood, the intensity of that anger will often be diminished.

The skills involved in listening include:

- Paraphrasing
- Asking questions, and
- Attentive silence

Paraphrasing

Imagine you're in an unresolved conflict in which the other person is adamantly arguing that her position is right (that is, using force). Perhaps you can't wait for her to stop talking so that you can tell her why she is wrong (use force back).

However, instead of doing what you might normally do, you paraphrase what she is saying, and you keep paraphrasing until she is satisfied that you have fully heard and understood her. In other words, you use her force, but don't use any of your own. Remember Newton's Law. Paraphrasing communicates to the other person that you really want to understand, and a paraphrase is your attempt to approximate what the other person has said. When you paraphrase, you don't have to worry about repeating verbatim; the important thing is that the other person knows that you are truly interested in understanding her position.

Each time you respond with a paraphrase, ask a verifying question like "Is that right?" or "Is that correct?"; i.e., "Did I understand you as you wanted to be understood?"

For example, let's say you've opened a conversation with one of your employees with the assertion that "I want you to contribute more to the team by helping those who are less experienced than you."

The other person responds with, "You say you want us to function as a team, but every time there's a decision to be made, you make it on your own and then tell me what I must do. That doesn't sound like teamwork to me."

In this situation, you might paraphrase by saying something like:

- "So what I hear you saying is that I say one thing and do another. Is that correct?" or,

- "You're saying that I demand teamwork from others but don't practice it myself. Is that right?"

You may also choose to paraphrase the underlying feeling being expressed by saying, "You seem to be angry with me? Am I right?"

Or let's say that your spouse confronts you with the following persuasive argument: "Just because you earn the money, you think I don't contribute anything valuable to this family."

In this marital scenario, you might paraphrase by saying "So you're not feeling appreciated for what you do. Is that correct?"

Or you may choose to paraphrase the feelings that have not been directly expressed: "That must make you feel angry when I do that. Is that right?"

In both cases, you have a choice: You can argue for your position by explaining why the other person's perception is wrong and yours is correct (in other words, you can use force against force) or you can give up your need to be right by paraphrasing what's being said to you. How you behave at this moment will determine whether the conflict escalates or gets resolved. It's why I maintain that if you're in a conflict with someone and it doesn't get resolved, *you're the one keeping the conflict going* by continually arguing for your position instead of listening.

And when you ask, "Is that correct?" or "Is that right?" you're asking if the other person thinks she has been *fully* understood. If, in response to this question, the person says "yes" (you have understood), you might follow with:

- "Is there anything else I should know?" or
- "Tell me more." or
- "What else?" or
- "Anything else you want to say?"

Keep paraphrasing and asking "Is that right?" until the person knows that you fully understand her position. This is extremely important, especially if you haven't been listening in the past. The other person will begin to move toward partnership, perceiving opportunities for bringing up many things that have been unexpressed until now. Keep paraphrasing so that even if she thinks you haven't cared in the past, she knows you care now.

One remarkable effect of this strategy will be that you will almost certainly notice that with each paraphrase the intensity with which the other person states her position will likely diminish. Because your paraphrasing communicates your willingness to listen and to give up your need to be right, your adversary will also gradually give up *her* need to be right and will become more willing to listen to you.

When you're sure that the other person realizes that you do, indeed, understand, summarize all that has been said and ask once again if your summary is accurate. If you get anything but a "yes", ask what is not accurate and continue paraphrasing until you hear that magic "yes" word in response to every point in the discussion. That's the moment at which you will be ready to move to the next step, which I call "bridging" and which you will learn about in Chapter 12.

As you are paraphrasing, be careful that your tone of voice conveys curiosity, not judgment or the threat of criticism. If your tone conveys anything negative, you will get the same thing in return, and the other person will not give up his need to be right. If you are paraphrasing accurately but the other person continues to seem defensive, it may be because your tone of voice sounds judgmental.

You may be reluctant to use paraphrasing, thinking that it will lead the other person to think that you agree with him. Certainly, if you don't agree but the other person seems to behave as though you do, you must make it clear that you're not agreeing, you're merely listening to make sure you understand.

At the same time, you must also be open to the possibility that you will see the validity of the other's position and end up agreeing after all. Always bear in mind (recall Chapter 2) that one of the conditions of giving up the need to be right is the willingness to concede that the other person is right—from her perspective.

Asking Questions

Paraphrasing may significantly reduce the emotional attachment to being right, but that technique may not uncover another person's needs. It's possible that, in response to one of your paraphrases, the other person will say, "Let me tell you what I need", but it's more likely that to uncover the need you'll have to ask one or more questions.

The kind of questions I encourage you to ask are called "open-ended"—questions that encourage the other person to reveal what's going on, as distinct from "closed-ended" questions that require only a "yes" or "no" answer.

Have you ever been stopped for speeding? Imagine the traffic officer approaching your car after pulling you over. You open your window and search for your driver's license. The traffic officer asks you:

"Is this your vehicle?"

"Do you have your driver's license and registration?"

"Have you been drinking?"

"Do you know how fast you were going?"

"Will you please remain in your car?"

What's common to these questions? Every one is closed-ended. The officer is trying to leave you as little room as possible for maneuvering. As Jack Webb used to say on the old Dragnet television show, "Just the facts, ma'am, just the facts."

You may want to elaborate on your "yes" or "no" with a statement like "No officer, I didn't know how fast I was going, but I couldn't have been going over the speed limit because . . .", but that's your choice, and the officer isn't really wanting you to do that and may even interrupt to stop you from talking. Hence, the closed-ended questions.

Similarly, when you ask "yes or no" questions in a situation where conflict is present, the other person may become defensive, thinking that she is being interrogated.

For example, someone may seek your advice about how to deal with a problem and you may ask, "Have you talked to your boss about this?" What you're really saying is, *"You should talk to your boss."*

When you ask your children after punishing them, "Have you now learned your lesson?" you're really telling your children that *they'd better change or they'll be punished again.*

When you say to a friend whose boyfriend just broke up with her, "Isn't this exactly what happened with your previous boyfriend?" you're really trying to demonstrate to your friend that she keeps repeating the same relationship mistakes.

Moreover, when people feel backed into a corner by closed-ended questions, they may lie or distort the truth to protect themselves. ("I couldn't have been speeding, officer. My speedometer showed I was going 58 not.70.")

Of course, closed-ended questions have their place. I've already suggested that, after paraphrasing, you ask, "Is that correct?" which is, of course, a closed-ended question that you are using to confirm the validity of the information you have just paraphrased.

When you want to resolve a conflict, do not use closed-ended questions to "lead" the other person into responding as you would like him to. All of us know when we're being "sold" versus when we're being listened to. Be sure you're listening and not selling. If you find, as you are listening, that the other person is not forthcoming with information or is still being defensive, check out the kinds of questions you are asking. It's likely that you're asking mostly closed-ended questions. If people are continuing to be defensive, you're probably causing them to think there's something they have to defend.

Open-ended questions, on the other hand, give the responder the freedom to answer as expansively as she chooses. They are less likely to be perceived as manipulative or as an attempt to direct the responder to answer in a particular way.

Open-ended questions typically begin with either "what" or "how" or "why". Many people do not like to begin questions with "why" because such an opening may produce a defensive answer. Although there's some validity to that—and you should pay attention to the other person's response to "why" questions—I believe the key is that a "why" question can yield useful information as to how a person thinks and the reasons he thinks that way *provided that it's asked in a truly curious tone of voice and visually accompanied by a facial expression that is consistent with the notion of curiosity rather than accusation.*

A good example of this is the question we brought up earlier, "Why is this important to you?" This sort of question, sincerely asked, can produce an understanding of what the other person needs.

Here are a few examples of how you might use the combination of paraphrasing and open-ended questions to uncover the needs of the other person in a conflict situation. It would perhaps be helpful for you to read these examples aloud and to practice using a curious tone of voice rather than a judgmental tone as you do so.

Example 1:

You've been waiting for your supplier to deliver some parts that are needed by one of your customers. You have some of the parts, but not all that your customer needs. You want your boss to ask the customer to extend a deadline for delivery of the parts you don't have so that your department can ship a complete order versus a partial one.

You (persuading): If we get an extension, it will give our supplier time to get the missing parts and the customer won't have to deal with two separate shipments from us.

Boss: No. I don't think we should do that.

You (open-ended question): Why not?

Boss: Because this is a new customer and we have to establish our credibility by getting the shipment to them when we said we would even if it means two separate shipments.

You (paraphrase): So you're concerned about our credibility, is that right?

Boss: Absolutely.

You (open-ended question): What other reason might you have for not wanting to request a deadline extension?

Boss: That's the only one.

You can see that "credibility" is the boss's need, and your questioning and paraphrasing have uncovered it even though your boss originally said "no".

In this example, I'm assuming that the boss's "no" didn't sound like *take it or leave it*. If it had, then you should test this before proceeding, using a question like "Are you open to considering other options?"

Example 2:

You (assertion): I want you to contribute more to the team by helping those who are less experienced than you.

Employee: You say you want me to be more of a team player. But every time there's a decision to be made, you make it on your own and then tell me what I must do. That doesn't sound like teamwork to me.

You (paraphrase): You're saying that I demand teamwork from others but don't practice it myself. Is that right?

Employee: That's right. Why should I help others when you seem to ignore me?

You (paraphrase): So you get frustrated when I make these requests but don't ask you what you think. Is that correct?

Employee: That's right.

You (expressing appreciation): Thank you for telling me. **(open-ended question)** What else should I know?

Employee: That's it.

You (open-ended question): What would you like me to do?

Employee: Ask for my input into decisions before you make a final decision.

The employee's need to provide input into decisions has been easily and quickly uncovered by your willingness to listen non-defensively and without judgment. Had you chosen to defend yourself, the employee would probably have become defensive, and the conflict might have escalated even further.

Example 3:

A co-worker has been late in getting some information to you that you need for a report. This has happened before and you want the co-worker to commit to getting information to you when it's due.

> **You (inspiration)**: I feel like I'm rowing the boat with only one oar. I'm going around in circles and not getting anywhere. **(assertion)** I want you to pick up the other oar and row with me.
>
> **Co-worker**: I just can't get you the information you need when you need it.
>
> **You (open-ended question)**: Why not?
>
> **Co-worker:** I just have so many other things to do. I don't have enough time in the day to get everything done.
>
> **You (paraphrase)**: It must be frustrating to be unable to fill everyone's requests. Is that right?
>
> **Co-worker**: It is.
>
> **You (paraphrase)**: So it's not that you don't want to, it's just that there aren't enough hours in the day to do it all. Right?
>
> **Co-worker**: Absolutely.
>
> **You (open-ended question)**: How can I help?
>
> **Co-worker**: Get me more hours in the day.
>
> **You**: If I could, I would. **(open-ended question)** What else would help?
>
> **Co-worker**: Well, it always seems as though just as I'm beginning to work on your request, some emergency request comes in from my boss and I have to drop everything and respond to him.
>
> **You (paraphrase)**: So your boss often causes you to miss my deadline. Right?
>
> **Co-worker**: That's right.
>
> **You (open-ended question)**: What else makes it difficult for you to get information to me?
>
> **Co-worker**: That's it. If I had a way to deal with my boss, I'd be able to get you what you need.

By listening without judgment, you have discovered that your co-worker really does want to provide the information you need by the deadline. However, he needs a way to work more effectively with his boss. Had you instead chosen to use force and demanded that your requests be honored, your co-worker might have dug in his heels even more.

Here are two examples not related to work to demonstrate how the same skills might be used in your personal life.

Example 1:

In this example, you'd like your spouse to go to a classical music concert with you, but she says, "No, I'm not interested."

You (open-ended question): Why not?

Spouse: Because that kind of music bores me.

You (paraphrase): So it's not the concert itself, it's the music you don't like. Is that correct?

Spouse: Yes.

You (open-ended question): What other reasons do you have for not wanting to go?

Spouse: I'm too tired to go to a concert in the evenings.

You (paraphrase): So evening concerts are hard after a tiring day, correct?

Spouse: Yes.

You (open-ended question): Anything else?

Spouse: No, that's it.

Can you see that the spouse does not object to going to a concert but simply to the type of music and the fact that it's at the end of the day? (Have you noticed that closed-ended question?). The spouse's needs relate to finding a concert she likes and one she can go to when she's not tired.

These concerns are easily handled if you listen to find out what they are. If, however, you try to argue for why you're right and your spouse is wrong, then you're in for a very long night.

Example 2:

In the following scenario, your spouse confronts you:

Spouse: Just because you earn the money you think I don't contribute anything valuable to this family.

You (paraphrase): So you're not feeling appreciated for what you do. Is that correct?

Spouse: Exactly

You (paraphrase): And when I do that, it really makes you angry, right?

Spouse: Damn right.

You (open-ended question): What can I do to make it up to you?

Spouse: You can start with an apology.

You (open-ended question): Anything else?

Spouse: You can tell me how much you appreciate me every once in a while.

You (open-ended question): Anything else?

Spouse: How about putting your dishes in the dishwasher.

You (open-ended question): Anything else?

Spouse: No. That's a good start.

Now imagine for a moment what might happen in this same scenario if instead of listening you talked about how hard you work and it's your spouse who should appreciate you.

A good place to use open-ended questions is when the other person uses some word that might contain emotion. Ask your question based on that emotional word. Remember, the conflict is kept in place by one's emotional attachment to being right. Uncovering this emotional attachment and talking about it may move the conflict towards resolution. Here are some examples (I've highlighted the emotional word):

Other person: I am so **frustrated** by this conversation.

You: What frustrates you? Or Why?

Other person: I'm **not really comfortable** with the decision.

You: Why are you uncomfortable?

Other person: I'm having a **tough** time coming up with ideas.

You: What's tough about it?

Other person: You make it **really hard** to agree with you.

You: How do I make it hard? (Or, What do you mean?)

Other words to listen for because of their emotional content include:

- Upset
- Overwhelmed
- Embarrassed
- Angry
- Afraid
- Irritated
- Annoyed

When you hear these words, paraphrase to communicate that you understand the emotion, and then ask a question to determine why the person is experiencing these emotions.

Attentive Silence

Have you ever had the experience of having someone tell you she's listening to you while she checks her email, writes a note and/or fumbles through her desk looking for something? How do you feel? Do you really believe you're being listened to?

It's not only important that you communicate your willingness to listen using paraphrasing and open-ended questions. It's also important that your words, body posture, and facial expressions are consistent with your verbal signals; every facet of your presence should communicate a message that says "I'm listening". If you find that you are paraphrasing and asking open-ended questions and still the other person is reluctant to respond, check out the rest of what's going on with you; the other person's reluctance or negativity may be happening because of your *nonverbal* behavior.

Here are some behaviors that will create the perception that you are truly listening:

- Look at the person. Eye contact supports listening.

- Put all other activities aside. Don't check email, don't write, put down the remote control. Give your full attention to the person.

- Get physically close to the other person without invading his or her "space" (usually determined by the length of a handshake). If you want to communicate the message "I'm on your side", sit beside the person, or if that 's not possible, lean slightly forward. The idea here is that physical closeness encourages psychological closeness.

- If it's appropriate, smile to communicate interest.

- Raise your eyebrows and nod to communicate understanding and interest.

Sometimes, you may really want to listen, but your mind wants to wander. When you notice this, refocus on the conversation by paraphrasing to yourself what you are hearing the person say.

COACHING TIPS FROM CHAPTER 10:

1. Any response other than "yes" to your question, "Will you do it?" should be heard as "I disagree."

2. Listening is a means for handling resistance and includes:

   A. Paraphrasing:

   - Communicates your sincere desire to understand another's position.
   - Ends by confirming that you did understand ("Is that correct?").

   B. Asking Questions:

   - Closed ended questions call for a yes/no response and may create defensiveness.
   - Closed ended questions are appropriate to confirm information. For example, asking, "Is that correct?" after a paraphrase.
   - Open-ended questions encourage an expansive response.

   C. Attentive Silence:

   - Communicates "I'm listening."

ASSIGNMENTS FROM CHAPTER 10

Have at least three separate conversations with people in your life in which *all you do* is paraphrase, ask open-ended questions and communicate, through your attentive silence, that you are interested in what they have to say. In particular, listen for words that seem to have an underlying emotion.

> *These conversations should **not** be with people with whom you're in an unresolved conflict. As I noted in the Introduction, I recommend waiting to approach the subjects of active conflict until you've finished the entire book. The purpose of these conversations is simply to practice listening.*
>
> *Tell these people that you're practicing an assignment from a book you're reading so that they don't distrust you when all you do is listen without stating your opinion.*
>
> *Schedule these conversations. Don't let them just happen. The danger is that if you wait for them to "just happen" they will never happen.*

Optional assignment: Write down your thoughts and feelings about your conflicts. You may choose to use the space below or to create a separate journal.

Remember: As your coach, I'm not asking you to agree with me. I am asking you to temporarily put aside your judgments and opinions and simply do the assignments.

TODAY'S DATE: _____

Thoughts and Feelings:

_____

_____

_____

_____

_____

_____

_____

_____

_____

_____

_____

_____

_____

_____

_____

_____

_____

_____

_____

_____

_____

_____

Chapter 11

Time Out:
Have You Been
Fully Underſtood?

Before proceeding to the next step, you want to be sure that you have been fully understood by the other person. You may have spent a considerable amount of time listening for the other person's needs and you want to make sure that your needs are understood as well. As the book title states, *"Everyone Wins!"* The title is not *"Everyone Wins... Except You."* You must make sure you get your needs met as well.

After the other person knows that he has been fully heard and understood, if you are at all concerned that you have not been fully heard and understood, ask the other person to paraphrase his understanding of your needs. For example, you might say:

- "What do you understand my needs to be?"
- "Will you please tell me what you heard me say about my needs?" Or simply
- "What did you hear me say?"

If the other person's paraphrase of what you said is not accurate, restate your needs and request that the other person continue paraphrasing until you're sure you've been fully heard and understood.

This will, most likely, be comfortable to do if you and the other person are of equal power or if the other person has less power than you. However, it can be tricky if this person is your boss, a peer or a family member with whom you've been quarreling. With these people, try a little "inoculation".

In medical terms, an inoculation is a way to ensure you don't get a disease. But in interpersonal terms, an inoculation is a way to reduce the discomfort that may accompany asking another person to paraphrase your needs.

For example, suppose you want to be sure your boss has understood you. You might say **(inoculation)**, "I don't mean in any way to upset you, and it's important to me that I know you understand me. Will you please tell me what you heard me say?"

Or you might say to a peer **(inoculation)**, "I hope you don't think I'm disrespecting your opinion. I just want to be sure you know what I mean. Will you please tell me what you think I mean?"

My wife and I were once arguing and she was getting frustrated because I clearly wasn't listening to her. I was becoming angry, and she knew that if she demanded I listen to her it would just make me angrier.

With as gentle a voice as possible, she said **(inoculation)**, "Larry, I really feel that you usually do listen to me. I don't think you are right now. Will you please just tell me what you think I'm saying?" How could I resist?

COACHING TIPS FROM CHAPTER 11:

1. This game is about "Everyone Wins!" . . . so be sure you have been fully heard and understood by the other person.

2. After the other person knows he has been fully heard and understood, make sure you have been fully heard and understood by asking the other person to paraphrase his understanding of what you have said.

3. If you're at all uncomfortable doing so, "inoculate" yourself against the discomfort.

ASSIGNMENTS FROM CHAPTER 11

Use the space below (or your private journal) to do the following:
1. Review your list of the people with whom you're in an unresolved conflict.

2. Select the people who you think have not fully heard and understood you.

3. For each person, write down the issue, topic, idea, position, want, need, etc. about which you think you have not been fully heard and understood.

Name:	Issue, topic, idea not heard?

Optional assignment: Write down your thoughts and feelings about your conflicts. You may choose to use the space below or to create a separate journal.

Remember: As your coach, I'm not asking you to agree with me. I am asking you to temporarily put aside your judgments and opinions and simply do the assignments.

TODAY'S DATE: _____

Thoughts and Feelings:

_____

_____

_____

_____

_____

_____

_____

_____

_____

_____

_____

_____

_____

_____

_____

_____

_____

_____

_____

_____

_____

_____

_____

_____

Chapter 12

Step 3:
Bridging:
Playing to Collaborate
Rather Than to Compete

Bridge. *n. A structure spanning and providing passage over a gap or barrier.*

The American Heritage Dictionary of the English Language

Initially, conflict often looks like a gap that simply cannot be bridged, a difference that no amount of work will remove. This is a scary notion, particularly in situations where conflict is not tolerable and cannot be sustained without doing irreparable harm.

Bridging is a technique that can reduce the emotional distance between you and another person so that conflict can be reduced to a manageable level or perhaps eliminated altogether.

During the bridging step, your objective is to make sure that you have, indeed, uncovered the other person's needs as well as your own and that it's now appropriate to begin looking for solutions.

All conflict is resolved based on one simple condition—"if X" (I meet your needs), "then Y" (you will meet my needs)—or vice versa. During this step, you will test the strength of this "if X, then Y" bridge.

Let's return to examples from earlier chapters. I'm going to recreate the conversations and, at the end, add the bridging statement that connects the two positions and moves the conversation forward.

Example 1:

You've been waiting for your supplier to deliver some parts that are needed by one of your customers. You have some of the parts, but not all that your customer needs. You want your boss to ask the customer to extend a deadline for delivery of the parts you don't have so that your department can ship a complete order versus a partial one.

You (persuading): If we get an extension, it will give our supplier time to get the missing parts and the customer won't have to deal with two separate shipments from us.

Boss: No. I don't think we should do that.

You (open-ended question): Why not?

Boss: Because this is a new customer and we have to establish our credibility by getting the shipment to them when we said we would even if it means two separate shipments.

You (paraphrase): So you're concerned about our credibility, is that right?

Boss: Absolutely.

You (open-ended question): What other reason might you have for not wanting to request a deadline extension?

Boss: That's the only one.

You (bridge): (If X) So if there were a way to have the deadline extended without losing credibility with the customer, (Then Y) will you ask the customer for that extension?

Boss: Perhaps. What are you thinking?

You (introducing brainstorming, step 4, Chapter 13): Let me make a suggestion...

Notice that the bridging question is *"will* you..." not *"would* you " or *"could* you." Remember, change requires a commitment to an act of will.

The fact is that you *want* the deadline extended. What is your *need*? Asking yourself *"Why is changing the deadline important to me?"* might yield an answer such as, "If my boss doesn't agree to help me get a deadline extension from the customer, I'll need help renegotiating with our supplier."

If this were the case, you might also bridge by asking, "If you'll help me find a way to convince our supplier to get the parts to us faster ("if X"), then we'd certainly be able to get them to our customer on time ("then Y"). Will you help me?"

Notice too that in this example, the boss said "perhaps", not "yes". This is a typical and completely appropriate response to a bridging question. After all, no solution is being offered, so it would be inappropriate to agree.

There are times, however, when in response to the bridging question, *"If I meet your need, will you meet mine?"* you will hear "yes". In that case, the conflict has been resolved and it is time to party (Chapter 15)!

There are other times, though, when your bridging question will get a "no" response. Recall that "no" either means there is still an un-met need, or it could be *take it or leave it*. You can uncover which it is simply by returning to the listening mode and asking "Are you open to talking about this? If the answer is "yes," ask an open-ended question like "What are your objections to what I'm suggesting?" If the answer is still "no," that's *take it or leave it*, so leave it and find alternative means for meeting your needs.

Example 2:

You (assertion): I want you to contribute more to the team by helping those who are less experienced than you.

Employee: You say you want me to be more of a team player. But every time there's a decision to be made, you make it on your own and then tell me what I must do. That doesn't sound like teamwork to me.

You (paraphrase): You're saying that I demand teamwork from others but don't practice it myself. Is that right?

Employee: That's right. Why should I help others when you seem to ignore me?

You (paraphrase): So you get frustrated when I make these requests but don't ask you what you think. Is that correct?

Employee: That's right.

You (express appreciation): Thank you for telling me. **(open-ended question)** What else should I know?

Employee: That's it.

You (open-ended question): What would you like me to do?

Employee: Ask for my input into decisions before you make a final decision.

You (bridge): (If X) So if I make sure and get your input before making any final decisions, (Then Y) will you help others on the team who have less experience?

Employee: I have to think about that.

You (open-ended question): What do you have to think about?

Employee: I'm not sure.

You (paraphrase): Let me guess. You're wondering if you can trust me in the future since I haven't done that in the past. Is that right?

Employee: I guess so. That sounds right.

You (bridge): Well let me just say that (If X) if you'll trust me, (Then Y) I promise not to betray your trust. **(open-ended question)** What do you think?

Employee: Okay it's a deal. I'm willing to see how it works out.

You (express appreciation): Thanks. It means a lot to me that you're willing to trust me even though I haven't been very trustworthy in the past. It's really great of you to agree in spite of that. **(celebrate the victory)** How about going to lunch together to seal the deal? My treat.

Employee: Sounds good.

In this example, you had to do more listening after the first bridge because the employee resisted the suggestion. Whenever you encounter resistance, return to listening.

As noted earlier, whenever an agreement is reached, it's important to "Express Appreciation" (Chapter 9) and "Celebrate the Victory" (Chapter 15).

Example 3:

A co-worker has been late in getting some information to you that you need for a report. This has happened before and you want the co-worker to commit to getting information to you when it's due.

You (inspiration): I feel like I'm rowing the boat with only one oar. I'm going around in circles and not getting anywhere. **(assertion)** I want you to pick up the other oar and row with me.

Co-worker: I just can't get you the information you need when you need it.

You (open-ended question): Why not?

Co-worker: I just have so many other things to do. I don't have enough time in the day to get everything done.

You (paraphrase): It must be frustrating to be unable to fill everyone's requests. Is that right?

Co-worker: It is.

You (paraphrase): So it's not that you don't want to, it's just that there aren't enough hours in the day to do it all. Right?

Co-worker: Absolutely.

You (open-ended question): How can I help?

Co-worker: Get me more hours in the day.

You: If I could, I would. **(open-ended question)** What else would help?

Co-worker: Well, it always seems as though just as I'm beginning to work on your request, some emergency request comes in from my boss and I have to drop everything and respond to him.

You (paraphrase): So your boss often causes you to miss my deadline. Right?

Co-worker: Yours and others. That's right.

You (open-ended question): What else makes it difficult for you to get information to me?

Co-worker: That's it. If I had a way to deal with my boss, I'd be able to get you what you need.

You (bridge): (If X) If we can find a way to deal with your boss, (Then Y) will you commit to getting the information to me on time?

Co-worker: Of course. But how?

You (introducing brainstorming): Let me make a suggestion...

Notice in this example that the co-worker has unconsciously bridged, offering a way to span the gap between his needs and yours: *"If I had a way to deal with my boss, I'd be able to get you what you need."*

Example 4:

You (assertion): I want to promote Joe to that open supervisor position in the customer service department.

Boss: You've got to be kidding. Joe doesn't have the leadership capabilities necessary for that kind of responsibility.

You (testing 'take it or leave it'): Are you saying there are no conditions under which you'd consider a promotion for Joe?

Boss: Not exactly. It's just that I don't think Joe is ready to take the job.

You (open-ended question): Well, what do you think Joe is lacking?

Boss: It's clear to me that he's just not assertive enough.

You (open-ended question): Why is it important that he be assertive?

Boss: He's going to have to face the hard customer issues that the customer service reps can't handle. That's going to require a toughness that Joe just doesn't have.

You (open-ended question): Are there any other reasons why you might object to promoting Joe?

Boss: Not that I can think of.

You (bridge): (If X) If Joe can prove to you that he has the toughness you're looking for, (Then Y) will you agree to promote him?

Boss: You'd have to prove it to me.

You (bridge): (If X) And if I prove it to you, (Then Y) will you promote him?

Boss: We'll see. How do you propose to have him prove it?

You (introducing brainstorming): Let me make a suggestion...

As I noted back in Chapter 4, when I first used this example, if the boss is adamant (*take it or leave it*), that Joe not be promoted to the open position, then you must ask yourself, "Why is it important to me for Joe to be promoted?" Perhaps the issue isn't Joe's promotion at all. Perhaps you simply **want** to promote Joe as a way to meet your **need** to reward a good employee. There are many ways to reward an employee (your need) without necessarily promoting him (your want).

In that case, the bridge with your boss might sound like this: (if X) *"If I had a way other than promotion to reward Joe for his good performance,* (then Y) *will you support me doing so?"*

Example 5:

This example involved a negotiation over the budget.

Co-worker (persuasion): Our department should get the budget increase in order to complete installation of the web site, to hire an additional customer service person and to provide more sales training for our sales force. Doing these things will make us more responsive to our customer's needs and increase revenue.

You (paraphrase): So doing these things will make a difference for our customers and for our bottom line. Correct?

Co-worker: Absolutely.

You (open-ended question): And specifically how will doing these things make us more responsive to our customer's needs and increase revenue?

Co-worker (annoyed): I've already told you. The web site will help us to increase sales, hiring an additional customer service person will ensure that customer's questions are answered and providing more training to the sales people will help them to close more sales.

You (inoculation): I apologize if I've upset you. I just wanted to be sure I understood you. **(bridge)** Let me ask you this question. (If X) If there were a way to increase sales, ensure that customer's questions are answered and help the sales people close more sales without necessarily increasing your budget (Then Y) will you have that conversation with me?

Co-worker (sarcastically): No.

You (open-ended question): Why not?

Co-worker: Why should I? We need the extra money.

You (persuasion): I'm asking you to consider it for the good of the company as a whole. **(bridge)** (*If X*) If we could save the money, (*Then Y*) we'd all benefit.

Co-worker: What are you proposing?

You (introducing brainstorming): Let me make a suggestion...

Following are two examples where the same skills might be used in one's personal life.

Example 1:

In this example, you'd like your spouse to go to a classical music concert with you, but she says, "No, I'm not interested."

You (open-ended question): Why not?

Spouse: Because that kind of music bores me.

You (paraphrase): So it's not the concert itself, it's the music you don't like. Is that correct?

Spouse: Yes.

You (open-ended question): What other reasons do you have for not wanting to go?

Spouse: I'm too tired to go to a concert in the evenings.

You (paraphrase): So evening concerts are hard after a tiring day, correct?

Spouse: Yes.

You (open-ended question): Anything else?

Spouse: No, that's it. It's enough, isn't it?

You (open-ended question): What is it about classical music that bores you?

Spouse: It moves so slowly. It puts me to sleep.

You (open-ended question): Anything else you don't like about classical music?

Spouse: I don't think so.

You (persuasion): How about this? Let me bring home some classical music I think you'd like. **(bridge)** (*If X*) If you think it's as exciting and invigorating as I think you will, (*Then Y*) will you go to a concert with me if there's similar music?

Spouse: Not if it's during the week.

You (adding to the bridge): And it's during a weekend. **(open-ended question)**: What do you think?

Spouse: Bring home the music. Then I'll decide.

Obviously, there needs to be additional conversation. However, the conflict has moved forward towards resolution.

Example 2:

> **Spouse**: Just because you earn the money you think I don't contribute anything valuable to this family.
>
> **You (paraphrase)**: So you're not feeling appreciated for what you do. Is that correct?
>
> **Spouse**: Exactly.
>
> **You (paraphrase)**: I've really made you angry, right?
>
> **Spouse**: Damn right.
>
> **You (open-ended question)**: What can I do to make it up to you?
>
> **Spouse**: You can start with an apology.
>
> **You (open-ended question)**: Anything else?
>
> **Spouse**: You can tell me how much you appreciate me every once in a while.
>
> **You (open-ended question)**: Anything else?
>
> **Spouse**: How about putting your dishes in the dishwasher.
>
> **You (open-ended question)**: Anything else?
>
> **Spouse**: No. That's a good start.
>
> **You (giving up the need to be right)**: First of all, I apologize from the bottom of my heart. **(assertion and express appreciation)** I want you to know how much I do appreciate you. **(bridge)** Next, (*if X*) If I do express my appreciation more frequently and put my dishes in the dishwasher, (*then Y*) will you forgive me?
>
> **Spouse**: I'll see. That's a good start.

This conflict demonstrates an important point about all conflict whether at work or at home. An apology, backed up by action, is an almost guaranteed way to move a conflict forward. It requires, of course, a willingness to give up the need to be right.

Coaching Tips From Chapter 12:

1. Bridge by asking "If X (if I meet your needs), then Y (Will you meet mine)?"

2. If the answer is "yes", express appreciation and celebrate.

3. Most often, the answer is a non-committal response such as "Perhaps" or "What do you propose?" This is appropriate because it gives you permission to move to the next step.

ASSIGNMENTS FROM CHAPTER 12

Use the space below (or your private journal) to do the following:

1. Review the list of the people with whom you're in an unresolved conflict.

2. For each person, write several potential "If X, Then Y" bridges that would meet his or her needs as well as yours.

3. Remember that you can't know for sure what will work until you actually have a conversation with these people. However, it's helpful to prepare for those conversations with some "if X, then Y" potential solutions.

4. Practice saying these words with your "live" coach. Saying them out loud (and getting feedback) will give you a better sense of their effectiveness than simply saying them to yourself.

Name	Bridge(s)

Optional assignment: Write down your thoughts and feelings about your conflicts. You may choose to use the space below or to create a separate journal.

Remember: As your coach, I'm not asking you to agree with me. I am asking you to temporarily put aside your judgments and opinions and simply do the assignments.

TODAY'S DATE: _____

Thoughts and Feelings:

_____
_____
_____
_____
_____
_____
_____
_____
_____
_____
_____
_____
_____
_____
_____
_____
_____
_____
_____
_____
_____

Chapter 13

Step 4:
Brainstorming:
There Are Many Ways
For Everyone
To Win the Game

In Chapter 2, I reiterated what my colleague, Michael, continues to emphasize: *it's a world of "and," not a world of "but"*. Brainstorming is where you explore all these possible "ands."

Once you have a "maybe" in response to your "if X, then Y" bridge, the next step is to **brainstorm together** to find as many options as possible for meeting the needs of everyone involved in the conflict. The transition from bridging to brainstorming is a statement such as, *"Let me make a suggestion"* or *"Let's talk about how to make that happen"*.

The key words in this step are *brainstorm* and *together*. As someone said to me recently, ***"An idea imposed is an idea opposed."*** You're looking for commitment, not compliance, as you would with *take it or leave it*. We already know and understand that if the other person doesn't feel she has been involved in the decision, she will find a way to sabotage the decision—no matter how much she may appear to agree.

Before you begin brainstorming, be prepared with some suggestions to offer, especially if you're the one who has initiated the conflict. After all, you're the one asking for the change. It's like getting water from a well: you may have to prime the pump to get the ideas flowing from the other person.

If you find that the other person is making suggestions and participating in the brainstorming, then the process is simple. As you are brainstorming, use paper, a flip chart, a board, a computer, etc. to *write down every idea offered.* It's important to establish an agreement that there be *absolutely no evaluation of suggestions* during this process and that you *take some time to explore further* before agreeing to implement the first idea presented. All ideas are okay—sometimes, the sillier the better— in order to free you up to creatively brainstorm.

Some people believe that writing down the "silly" ideas trivializes the process. I ask you to consider instead that following this rule actually spurs creativity. People must feel free to make mistakes in order to be creative. The greater the degree to which people feel free to be themselves, without being judged, the more creative they will be.

Additionally, when you write down *every* idea offered, you demonstrate the importance of what the person is saying. If you do this, you'll find that when it's time to "Choose the Everyone Wins Solutions," (next chapter), the other person will be more open to have his items removed from consideration, if need be.

For example, suppose you and your boss are brainstorming options to prove to your boss that Joe, an employee you want to promote, is sufficiently "assertive" to be promoted to a supervisor's position in the customer service department. As you're brainstorming, you smile and suggest that Joe come into your boss's office and pick a verbal fight with the boss. If Joe can handle the boss, you suggest, that would be proof of his assertiveness. You turn to the flip chart and write down, ***"Joe picks fight with boss. Winner takes all."***

Your boss gets in the spirit of things and suggests that he and Joe actually get into a boxing match with a referee who decides the winner. You dutifully write on the flip chart, ***"Boxing match. Referee declares the winner."*** In doing so, you're reinforcing the agreement that creativity is valued.

While neither one of these ideas is accepted, of course, it does lead to an idea to create a role play in which Joe demonstrates his assertiveness in handling difficult customer situations. You write "Role Play" on the flip chart.

The point is that the "role play" idea might not have occurred to either of you without first having some fun with the other, less realistic, ideas.

Or suppose you're brainstorming how to make sure sales reps close more sales without necessarily spending more money on training. You may offer the ideas to:

- Fire any sales rep who doesn't close more sales
- Get rid of customers who refuse to buy
- Sell the company
- Change the product line, etc.

You write these items down.

While you're not serious about these suggestions, of course, it does spur another suggestion: "Instead of firing them," you say, "suppose we turn it into a contest with the sales rep who closes the most sales receiving a prize?" (The idea being that perhaps the sales reps know how to close sales, but they aren't adequately rewarded when they do so).

The person you're brainstorming with likes that idea and adds, "How about this? Instead of making it a contest between individuals, let's put the sales reps into teams and have the team that closes the most sales get the prize. We'd give a prize to each member of the team with the increased sales revenue paying for the cost of the prizes. In that way, team members who are strong in closing will have the incentive to teach those on the team who are not as strong."

Again, notice that the "ridiculous" ideas helped to create the more realistic ones.

Or imagine that you and your spouse are brainstorming alternatives for concerts to attend and she suggests dressing in baggy shorts and baseball caps to attend a hip-hop concert rather than the classical concert you had wanted to attend. On a piece of paper you write down, "Hip-hop. Baggy shorts. Baseball caps."

While hip-hop may be the last kind of music you want to listen to, you realize that dressing up would be fun and suggest going to the classical concert and wearing formal attire, hiring a limo and going out to a great restaurant for dinner. You write down, "Formal clothes. Limo. Dinner."

The suggestion delights your spouse, who begins to get excited about going to hear classical music.

If you find that ideas are drying up, reread aloud the items on the list. Sometimes, as you're reading, other ideas will occur to you. As noted above, take time to allow ideas to emerge. If you cut off the brainstorming too quickly, you may limit the possibilities for creative solutions.

I've assumed in this that the person you're brainstorming with has been a willing participant. However, if you find that you're suggesting most of the solutions without much input from the other person, this indicates that the other person may not be invested in finding a solution. Perhaps there is some underlying emotion that has not yet been expressed and this withholding attitude on his part is his way of letting you know.

For instance, an example from the last chapter involved enlisting your boss's aid in asking a customer to extend a deadline for delivery of the parts you don't yet have so that your department can ship a complete order versus a partial one. The example ended with you saying, "Let me make a suggestion."

Suppose the conversation proceeded in this manner:

You: Let me make a suggestion. I have a great relationship with the purchasing manager at the company. Let me talk to him to see if I can convince him to wait on the complete order. What do you think?

Boss: I don't like it.

You (open-ended question): Why not?

Boss: I'm concerned that it might put doubt in her mind about our ability to ship future orders on time.

You (attempting to involve your boss in the brainstorming): What ideas do you have about how we can do it?

Boss: I don't have any.

You (bridge): *(If X)* If I can have a conversation with the purchasing manager without creating doubt about future orders, *(Then Y)* will you back me up?

Boss: I'm not sure.

You (open-ended question): What are you unsure about?

Boss: I just don't think it's possible.

You (open-ended question): What makes you say that?

Boss: It just doesn't feel right.

You (making a suggestion using persuasion): Let me just test this with the purchasing manager. I know I can pull it off. We've established really good rapport.

Boss: I just don't know.

Clearly, something is going on with your boss. In this situation, or any situation in which you're having difficulty involving others in brainstorming, do the following:

- Test to see if the other person is really in a *'take it or leave it'* position ("Are you open to continuing this conversation?"). Perhaps the person is not actually open to an "Everyone Wins" solution.

- Suggest taking a break and returning in some reasonable time period with both of you agreeing to return with several additional options. If, when you return, the person still has no ideas to offer:

- Return to "Listening" to find out why this might be. For example, *(asserting)* "I really want this to be a collaborative process and I've noticed that I'm not able to come up with any ideas you like and that you haven't offered any other thoughts. *(open-ended question)* Why is that?" (Notice that the question is open-ended, not "Is there a problem?" which would be closed ended and could be perceived as an interrogation rather than a question.)

- Use "attentive silence". Ask, "How would you solve it?" and then be silent. Simply ask your question and wait. If the silence goes on for more than one minute (an enormous amount of time), suggest the second option above: take a break, and return at an appropriate time with suggestions for meeting everyone's needs.

COACHING TIPS FROM CHAPTER 13:

1. Brainstorm together so that everyone is invested in finding a solution.

2. Be open to every suggestion and don't close off the session before all ideas have been exhausted.

3. Be prepared with one or two suggestions when you are the one seeking change.

4. If the other person seems to be resisting brainstorming, find out why before proceeding. Brainstorming must involve everyone to be effective.

ASSIGNMENTS FROM CHAPTER 13

Use the space below (or your private journal) to do the following:

1. Using the exercise from the last chapter, review the "if X, then Y," bridges that you wrote there.

2. For each "if X, then Y," brainstorm as many options as you can think of to meet your needs and the needs of everyone involved in the conflict. You may want to enlist your "live coach" to help you with this brainstorming.

3. Have fun and let the ideas flow.

Optional assignment: Write down your thoughts and feelings about your conflicts. You may choose to use the space below or to create a separate journal.

Remember: As your coach, I'm not asking you to agree with me. I am asking you to temporarily put aside your judgments and opinions and simply do the assignments.

TODAY'S DATE: _____

Thoughts and Feelings:

_____

_____

_____

_____

_____

_____

_____

_____

_____

_____

_____

_____

_____

_____

_____

_____

_____

_____

_____

_____

_____

_____

Chapter 14

Step 5:

Choose "Everyone Wins" Solution(s)

Looking at all the options from Step 4, you and the people involved in the conflict simply select the option(s) that will meet everyone's needs. While there are many techniques you might use to select these options, it's important for you and the people with whom you're in conflict to agree on the technique you will use before beginning this step.

Among the potential techniques are the following:

1. **Read the options aloud, discuss the pros and cons of each and together select the one(s) that meets everyone's needs. The goal is to choose based on consensus, not unanimity.**

People should be able to "live with" and be committed to implementation. They do not need to be in complete, 100% agreement with every solution.

For example, consider the situation from a previous chapter where your co-worker failed to get needed information to you because his boss interrupted him with emergency requests. In listening to this co-worker, you discover that his boss has never actually demanded that your co-worker do something immediately. Instead, his boss usually says he needs it quickly and your co-worker, wanting to make a good impression, drops everything and begins working on his boss's request.

Your co-worker, who is uncomfortable asserting himself, agrees to tell his boss when he can get to the boss's request instead of immediately dropping other work. In exchange, you agree to give the co-worker even more of a lead-time on the information you need. While this may mean some extra work for you, you agree to do it in the interests of being sure you get the information you need from your co-worker. This is an agreement you both can "live with."

Or imagine that your spouse, who didn't want to go to a classical concert, agrees to go if you will get the limo, arrange for the dinner and make sure that the children's babysitter gets to your house and home again. You decide that this is an agreement you can live with.

2. Post all the options on flip charts and tape the flip charts to the wall.

Give everyone three votes represented by check marks. Each person puts a check mark beside the option(s) they prefer. A person could put three check marks beside one item, two beside one item and one beside another or divide the three check marks among three different options. The options with the most check marks are the ones to implement.

Prior to making a final decision, however, you may want to discuss these options further at this point to see if they can be modified to become even more inclusive of everyone's needs.

3. Establish criteria for making a decision.

For example, you and the people involved in the conflict may want the final options selected to be:

- The least expensive
- Easiest to implement
- Most likely to satisfy the customer

- Those that require the fewest resources to implement
- Those that use proven technology versus a technology that hasn't been fully tested

Using a five point scale, with "1" being the most desirable and "5" being the least desirable, everyone rates each item against the criteria. The item(s) with the lowest average score(s) gets implemented.

Regardless of the technique, after the *"Everyone Wins"* solutions have been chosen, be sure that the agreement is clear and understood in the same way by everyone. Summarize the agreement and ask, "Is that correct?" to be sure the summary is accurate. If the agreement must be recorded, write it down and have everyone sign it. Give everyone a copy of the signed agreement.

The danger here is that so much time and energy have been invested in arriving at this point that no one wants to raise objections. However, if you have any inkling at all that there may be some problems down the road, be sure that these are addressed. Better to handle it now than to find out later that you have to renegotiate the whole agreement.

Even though more time may be taken here to be sure everyone is satisfied, because people will have invested so much time and energy in the solutions, the time to implement the solutions will be faster and the implementation will go more smoothly.

Therefore, once the agreement has been summarized and clarified to everyone's satisfaction, it's a good idea to ask, "What obstacle(s) do you see to the implementation of this agreement?" and to go through "Listening," "Bridging" "Brainstorming" and "Choose the **Everyone Wins** Solution(s)" to be sure these obstacles are handled and resolved.

COACHING TIPS FROM CHAPTER 14:

1. Get agreement on a method that will be used to choose the solution(s) that will be implemented.

2. After selecting the options that meet everyone's needs, summarize the agreement to be sure it is clearly understood.

3. Be sure that any concerns about implementing the agreement are discussed before ending.

ASSIGNMENTS FROM CHAPTER 14

Use the space below (or your private journal) to do the following:

1. Go back to the options you developed in Chapter 13.
2. Select the options that you believe will best meet your needs as well as the needs of the people with whom you're in conflict.
3. Share your thinking with your "live" coach.

Optional assignment: Write down your thoughts and feelings about your conflicts. You may choose to use the space below or to create a separate journal.

Remember: As your coach, I'm not asking you to agree with me. I am asking you to temporarily put aside your judgments and opinions and simply do the assignments.

TODAY'S DATE: _____

Thoughts and Feelings:

_____

_____

_____

_____

_____

_____

_____

_____

_____

_____

_____

_____

_____

_____

_____

_____

_____

_____

_____

_____

_____

_____

_____

Part 3:

The Post Game Wrap Up

Chapter 15

Celebrate the Victory

"Celebrate, celebrate, dance to the music."

"Celebration"
Kool and the Gang:

In Chapter 7, I asked you to plan for how you will celebrate this moment. Now is the time to execute your plan.

Celebrate *NOW!* with the people who have been your collaborators in arriving at this moment. Sincerely express your gratitude and your appreciation for their willingness to engage with you by having the celebration for which you had planned. You've earned it!

Perhaps you haven't yet resolved every conflict. Celebrate the ones you have resolved.

If none have been resolved, celebrate anyway. Even if you haven't done all the assignments or yet resolved all your conflicts, you've probably noticed that just reading this book has altered the way you behave with some of the people in your life. Celebrate that fact! You've given up the need to be right and that's a triumph well worth celebrating.

Some of us wait to celebrate until we have enough time or the moment is just right or when we can relax, like on a vacation. I have news for you that I'm sure you've already heard: you will never have enough time, the moment will never be just right, and vacations are just not frequent enough.

So if you are the kind of person who waits to celebrate, I encourage you to take a vacation now. And the vacation you'll take is a vacation from the way you've always been.

In the Introduction, I asked you to agree to let me be your coach, which I suggested means letting me interrupt your usual way of thinking and behaving. I further suggested that this really is the only possible reason why you might want to read further because "if you always do what you've always done, you'll always get what you've always got."

So choose to get something different for yourself right now. Celebrate!

COACHING TIP FROM CHAPTER 15:

Don't wait. Celebrate! You've earned it.

ASSIGNMENTS FROM CHAPTER 15

Do the following:

1. Celebrate with the person(s) with whom you've resolved your conflict(s).

2. Celebrate even if the conflicts haven't been resolved.

3. Just Celebrate!

Optional assignment: Write down your thoughts and feelings about your conflicts. You may choose to use the space below or to create a separate journal.

Remember: As your coach, I'm not asking you to agree with me. I am asking you to temporarily put aside your judgments and opinions and simply do the assignments.

TODAY'S DATE: _____

Thoughts and Feelings:

_____
_____
_____
_____
_____
_____
_____
_____
_____
_____
_____
_____
_____
_____
_____
_____
_____
_____
_____
_____
_____

Chapter 16

You Must Keep Practicing For Everyone to Keep Winning

Recently, I was having a conversation with a potential client who wanted to build a stronger team. She was asking me about the "Everyone Wins" process and if I thought that teaching the process to her team would make a difference.

I asked her a lot of open-ended questions about her team's needs and I paraphrased her responses to make sure I was hearing her accurately. I wanted to be able to advise her as to whether teaching the process to her team would meet the team's needs.

I thought I understood her fully, so I used persuasion and inspiration to explain how I thought the process would help her team. She seemed satisfied with what I said, but I could tell by her voice that she had some doubts.

I said, "It seems like there's something you're still not satisfied with. What is it?"

She paused for a moment and then said, "It all sounds great. But we've been through training programs before and what we learned hasn't lasted. How do I know that this one will be any different?"

I'm often asked this question. People wonder if the money and time they spend in a workshop or being coached will have the desired results immediately and into the future (you may have wondered the same thing as you considered paying your money for this book).

I always answer as I answered this woman: "No." I said. "This won't last beyond the seminar."

I stopped and waited for that to sink in. I could tell that she was surprised by my answer. I think she expected me to try and convince her that my seminar would be different.

After pausing for a few moments, I continued. "You have to understand. Nothing you learn ever lasts unless you keep practicing. Eventually any skill will atrophy. Do you remember when you were in elementary school and you forgot some arithmetic over the summer and had to "re-learn" it in the fall? And how much algebra or chemistry or biology do you really remember from high school? A pianist who doesn't practice will still be able to play the piano, but not at the same level as when he practices regularly. The same is true for any skill."

I also related a story told by a comedian named Don Novello, who had a routine in which he talked about "the five-minute university." In this university, you'd pay the full, four-year tuition but you'd only go to school for five minutes. However, in those five-minutes, you'd learn everything the average college graduate remembers five years after he graduates.

By this point, the woman who had asked, "Will this last?" got the point. I hope you do, too. The only learning that lasts is learning that is used over and over and over again. Let me tell you a story that illustrates this point.

Not long ago I was having dinner with my colleague, Michael, and I was telling him that my book was almost finished. I wanted him to read it and critique it. I very much wanted his feedback because I developed many of the concepts in this book along with him.

As I was asking him to critique the book, I said, "If we disagree about what should be included in the book and we can't resolve the conflict, I want you to let me win."

Michael looked at me and said, "Can't resolve our conflicts? I thought that's what the book was about!"

I laughed uproariously. Caught again! Once more, Michael was reminding me that we could use the material in this book to resolve our disagreements as long as I gave up my need to be right.

But beyond that, Michael was telling me that even I, with long experience using and teaching the material in this book, still need a coach from time to time to remind me to use these skills.

So I want to end by asking you the question I often hear, and it's a question only you (and I) can answer for ourselves: "Will you keep practicing and practicing and practicing so that "Everyone Wins?"

COACHING TIP FROM CHAPTER 16:

You must keep practicing for these skills to be useful for the rest of your life.

ASSIGNMENTS FROM CHAPTER 16

Do the following:

1. Practice!

2. Review the list of the people with whom you're in an unresolved conflict.

3. Have a conversation with each person with the intention of resolving the conflicts so that "Everyone Wins." Use the skills you've learned in this book to do so.

Optional assignment: Write down your thoughts and feelings about your conflicts. You may choose to use the space below or to create a separate journal.

Remember: As your coach, I'm not asking you to agree with me. I am asking you to temporarily put aside your judgments and opinions and simply do the assignments.

TODAY'S DATE: _____

Thoughts and Feelings:

_____

_____

_____

_____

_____

_____

_____

_____

_____

_____

_____

_____

_____

_____

_____

_____

_____

_____

_____

_____

_____

_____

About the Author

Larry Barkan was born and raised in Chicago, and after graduating from Northeastern Illinois University, he became a high school teacher in the Chicago Public Schools, where he first began formulating his approach to conflict resolution.

Larry brought his philosophy of handling conflict to the business world in 1979, becoming a manager at American Hospital Supply Corporation (AHSC).

From 1979 until 1984, Larry held management consulting and training positions at corporate and division levels of AHSC, developing and delivering training programs to supervisors, managers and executives as well as providing coaching to leaders who were looking to enhance their impact, influence and overall leadership effectiveness.

Larry started his own consulting practice, Barkan Associates, in 1984 and in 1992 he co founded Executive Resources Consulting Group. In 2003, Larry became a Partner in The *Pivotal* Factor, LLC a firm dedicated to helping leaders achieve breakthrough results.

Larry and his wife have lived in the metropolitan Phoenix area since 1986.

☯

If you'd like to know more about the processes and programs offered by Larry Barkan and The Pivotal Factor, LLC please visit The Pivotal Factor web site at www.thepivotalfactor.com.

Larry is available for speeches, coaching and seminars and can be reached at ljbarkan@thepivotalfactor.com.

If you'd like to subscribe to Larry's email newsletters, E-mail him at the same address. The newsletters are distributed bi-weekly.

www.ingramcontent.com/pod-product-compliance
Lightning Source LLC
Chambersburg PA
CBHW021158010426
R18062100001B/R180621PG41931CBX00022B/39